You Raise Me Up
SONGS OF INSPIRATION

Produced by
Alfred Music Publishing Co., Inc.
P.O. Box 10003
Van Nuys, CA 91410-0003
alfred.com

Printed in USA.

No part of this book shall be reproduced, arranged, adapted, recorded, publicly performed, stored in a retrieval system, or transmitted by any means without written permission from the publisher. In order to comply with copyright laws, please apply for such written permission and/or license by contacting the publisher at alfred.com/permissions.

ISBN-10: 0-7390-8455-0
ISBN-13: 978-0-7390-8455-7

Cover Photo of leafy branch: © iStockphoto / Dole08

 Alfred Cares. Contents printed on 100% recycled paper.

Contents

Title	Page
Amazing Grace	3
Because You Loved Me	12
Bridge over Troubled Water	4
The Dance	8
From a Distance	17
The Greatest Love of All	22
Heal the World	30
Hero	27
(Your Love Is Lifting Me) Higher and Higher	34
I Believe in You	38
Live Like You Were Dying	46
Love Will Always Win	42
Man in the Mirror	51
The Prayer	92
The River	56
To Where You Are	60
Up Where We Belong	64
What a Wonderful World	68
Will You Be There (Radio Edit)	72
The Wind Beneath My Wings	76
You Haven't Seen the Last of Me	80
You Light Up My Life	84
You Raise Me Up	87

BRIDGE OVER TROUBLED WATER

Words and Music by Paul Simon
Arranged by Dan Coates

© 1969 (Renewed) PAUL SIMON (BMI)
All Rights Reserved

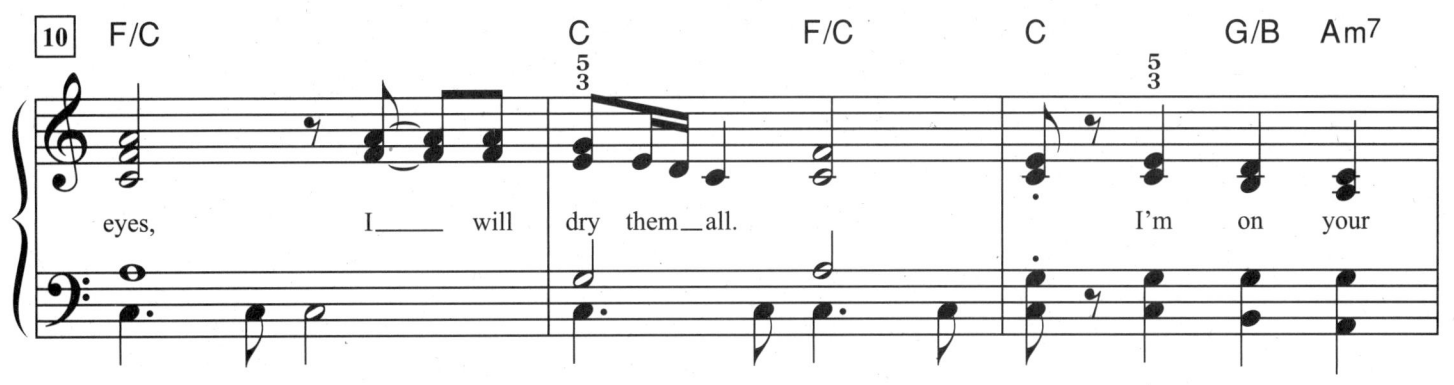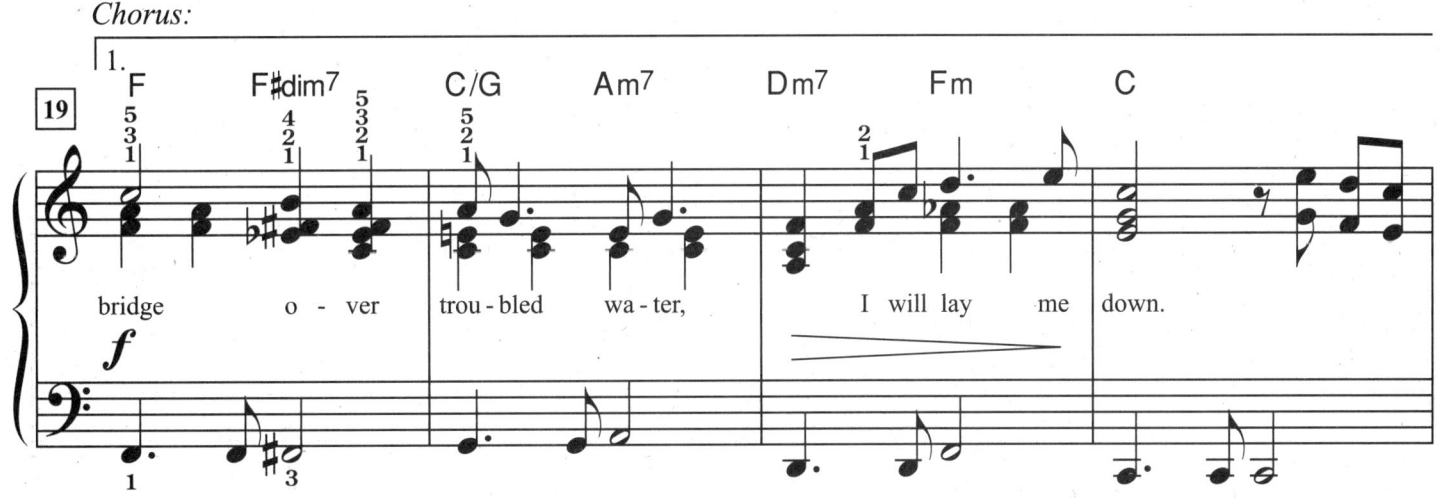

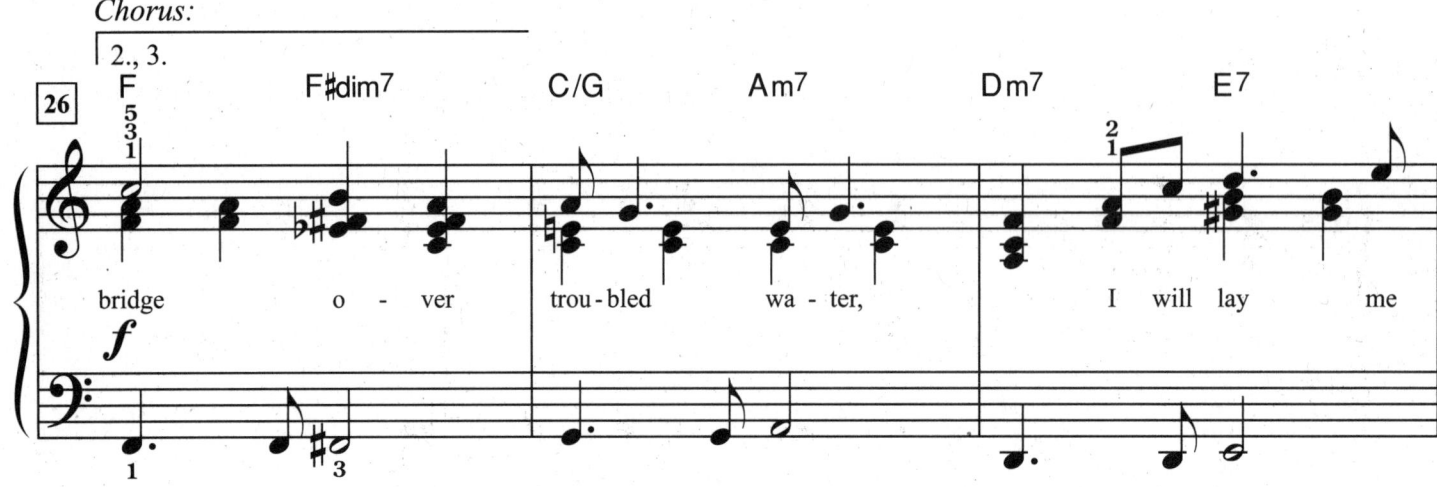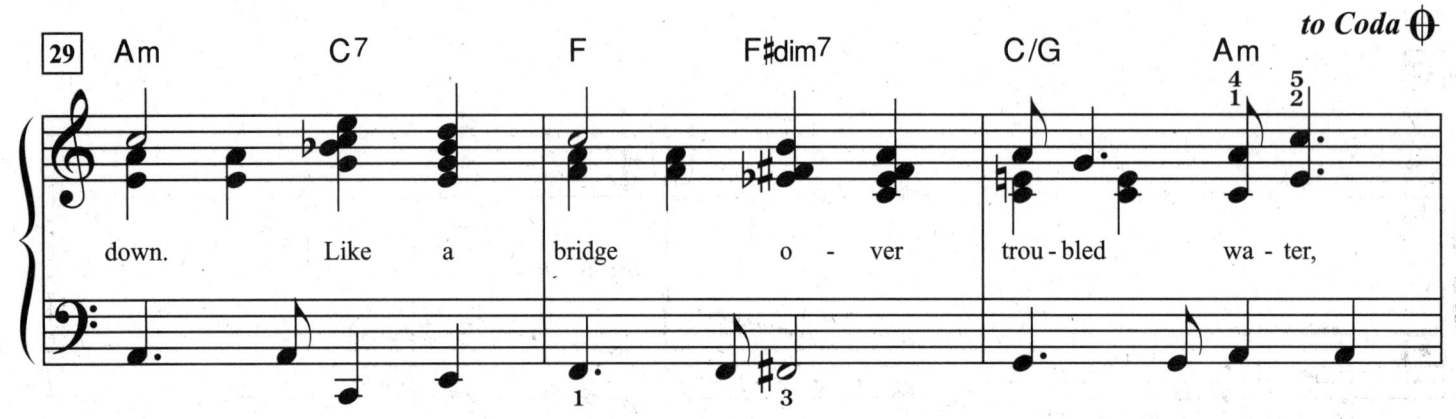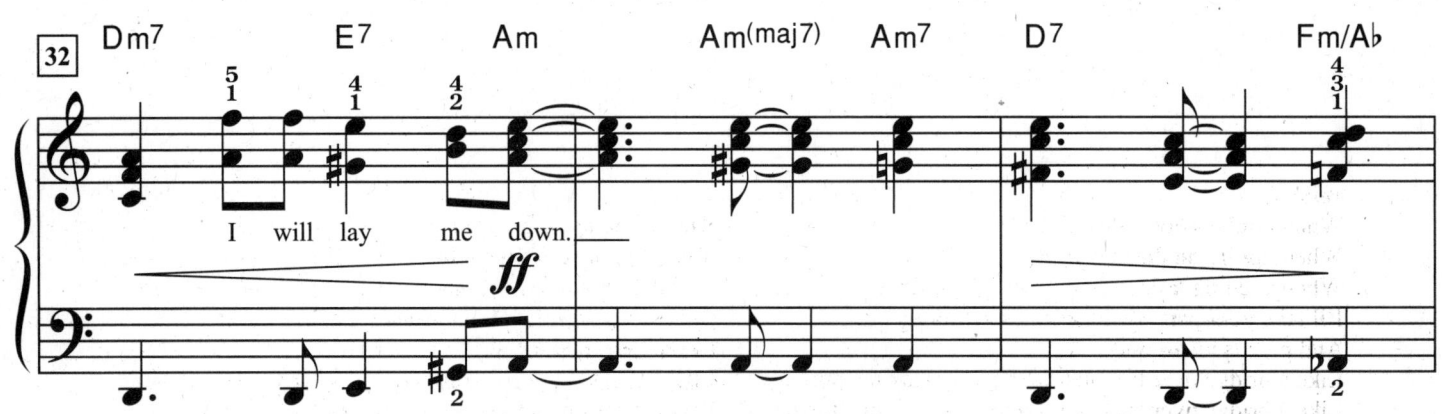

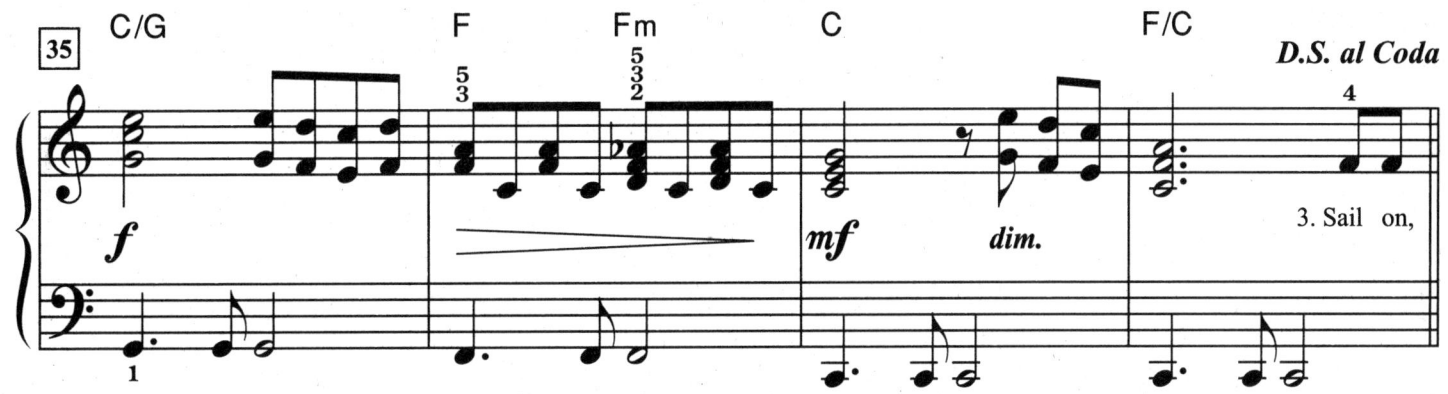
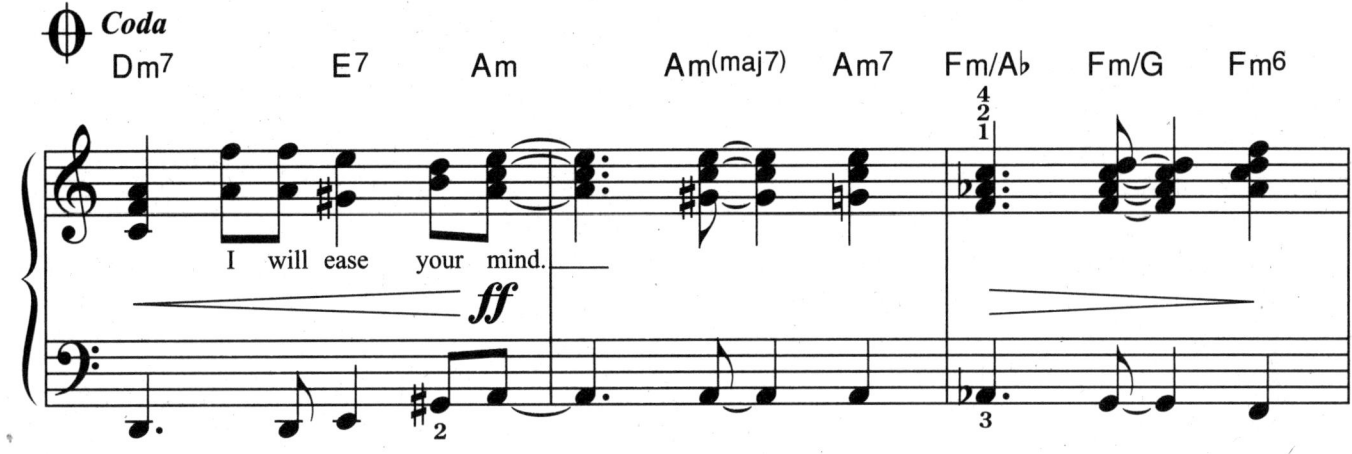
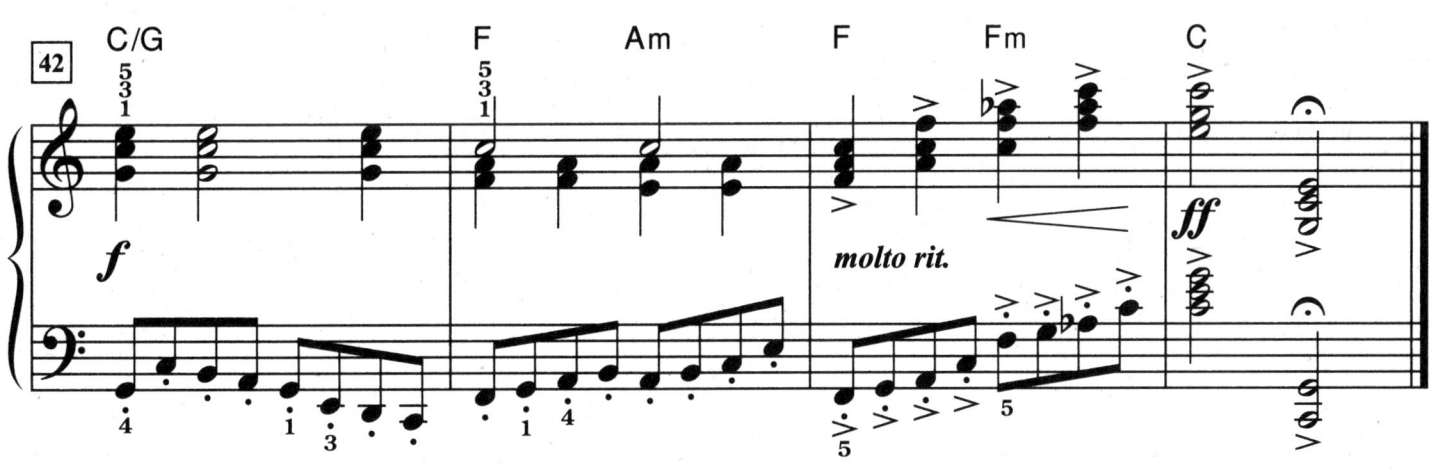

Verse 2:
When you're down and out,
When you're on the street,
When evening falls so hard, I will comfort you.
I'll take your part when darkness comes
And pain is all around.
Like a bridge over troubled water, I will lay me down.
Like a bridge over troubled water, I will lay me down.

Verse 3:
Sail on, silver girl, sail on by.
Your time has come to shine,
All your dreams are on their way.
See how they shine, if you need a friend.
I'm sailing right behind.
Like a bridge over troubled water, I will ease your mind.
Like a bridge over troubled water, I will ease your mind.

THE DANCE

Words and Music by Tony Arata
Arranged by Dan Coates

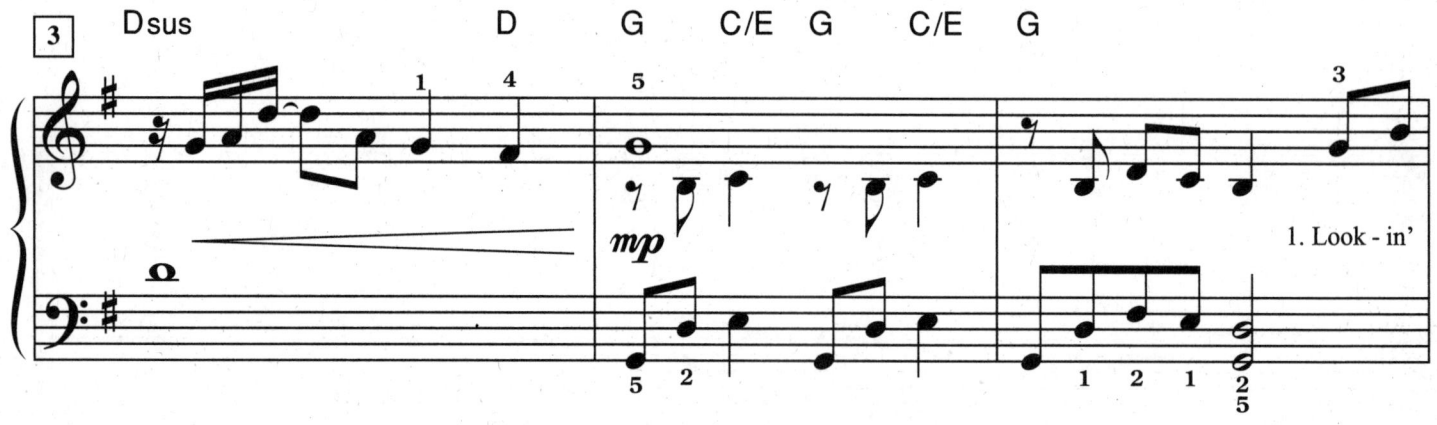

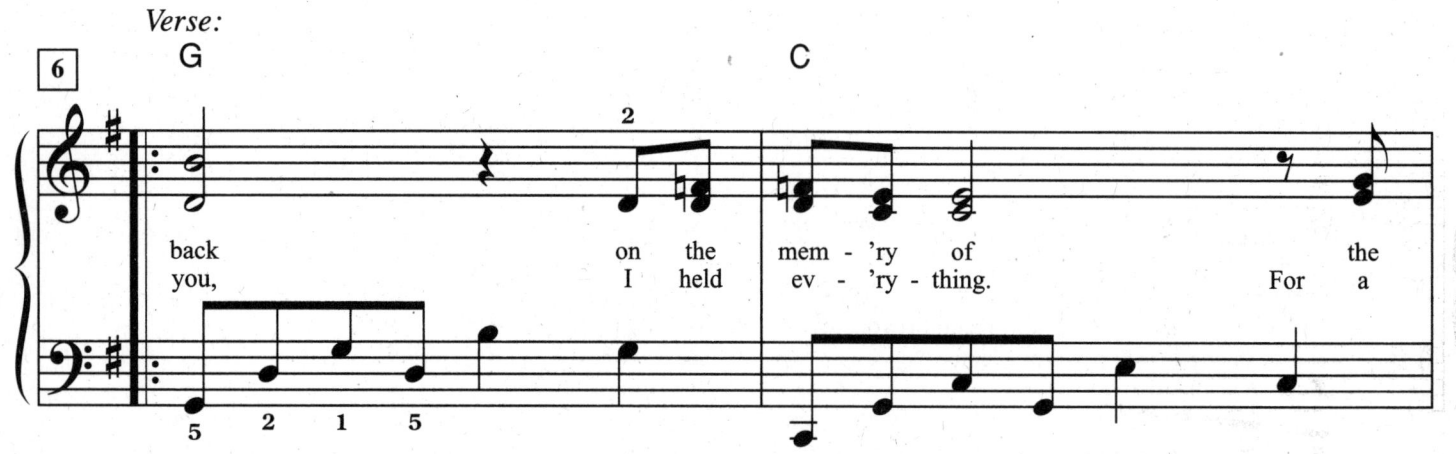

© 1989 MORGANACTIVE SONGS, INC. and EMI APRIL MUSIC INC.
All Rights Administered by Morgan Music Group Inc.
All Rights for the World Outside of North America Administered by WB MUSIC CORP.
All Rights Reserved

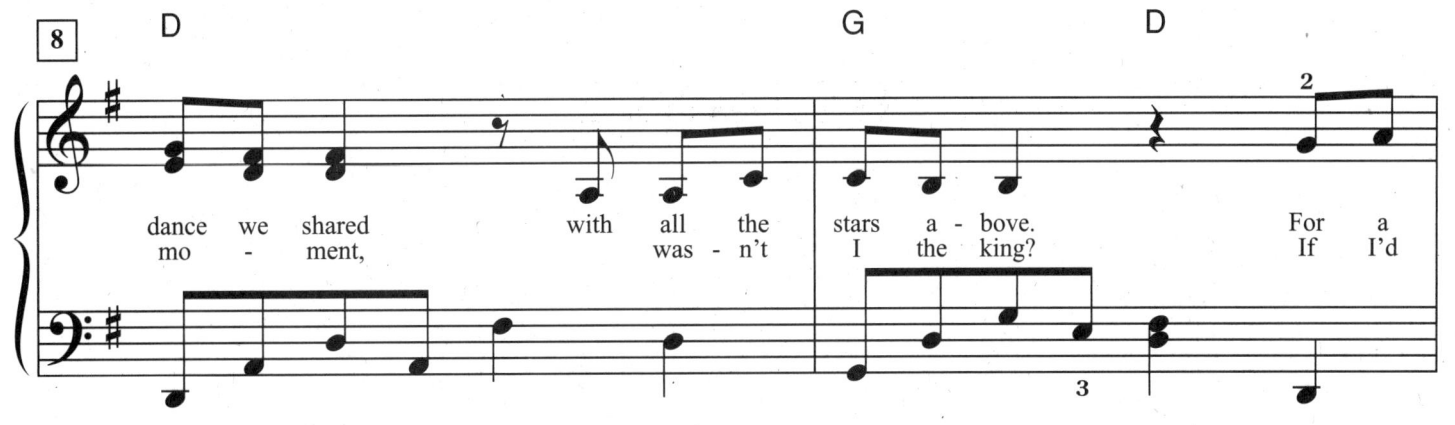

Chorus:

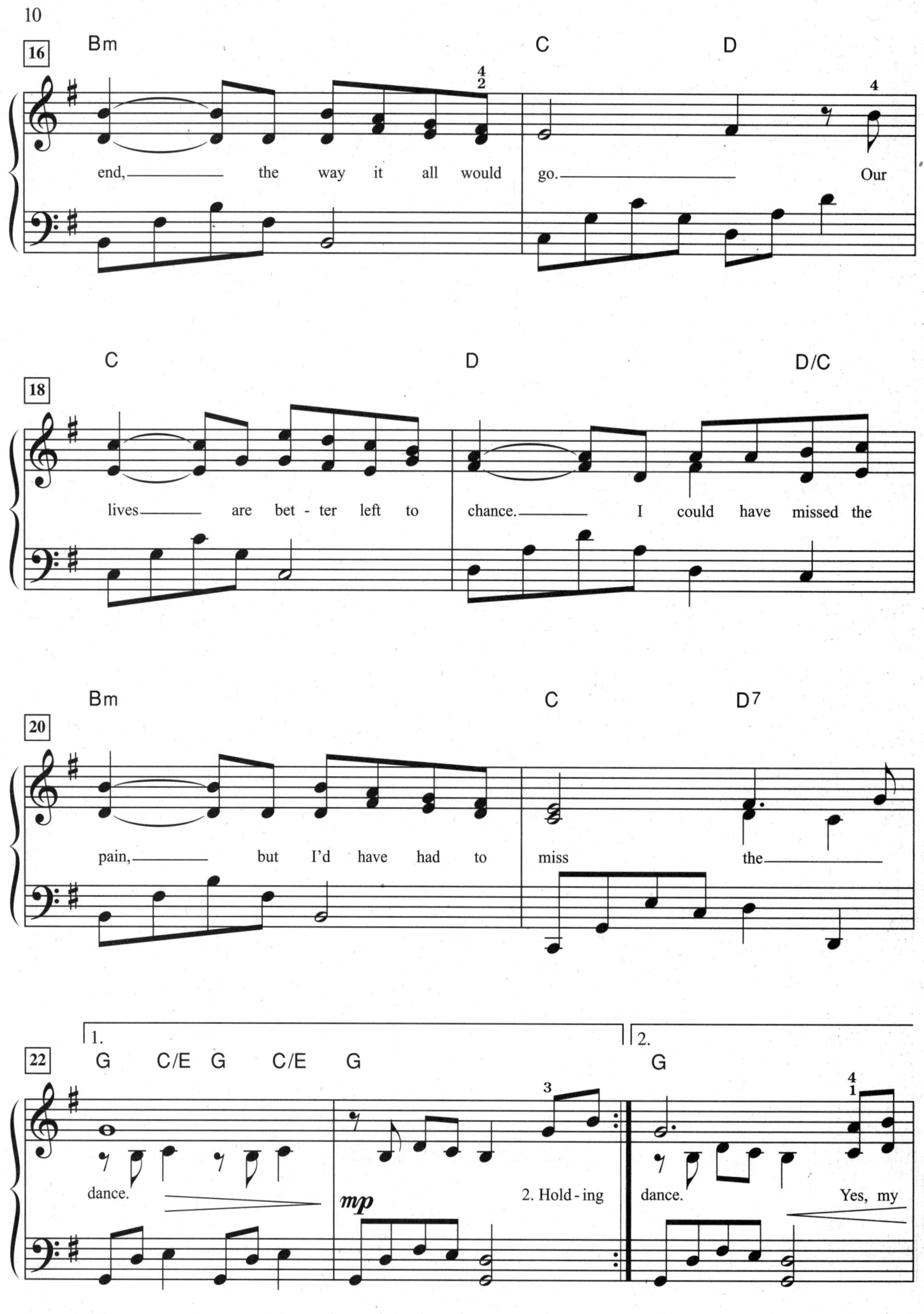

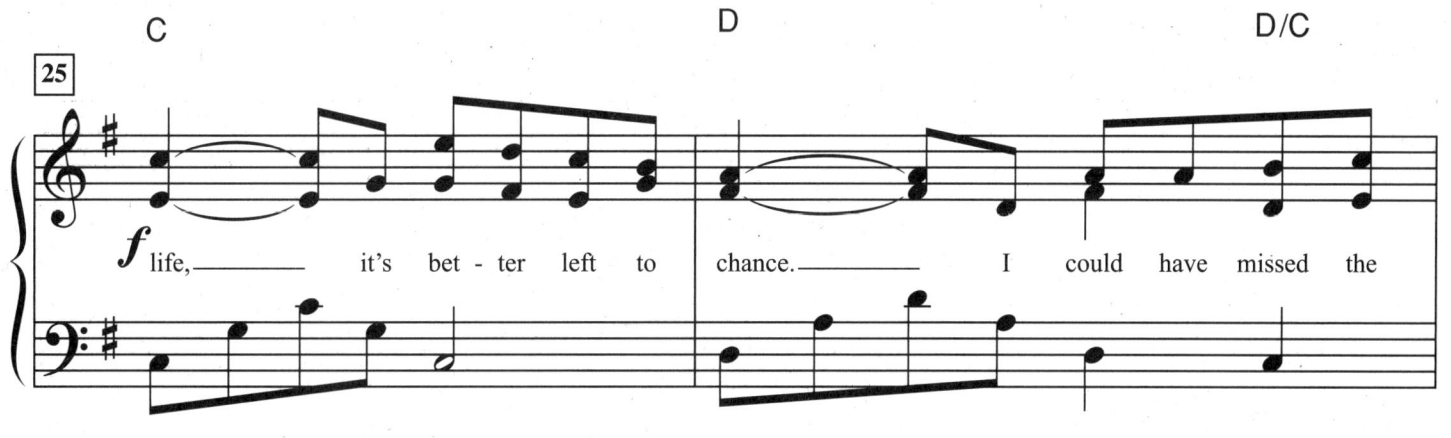
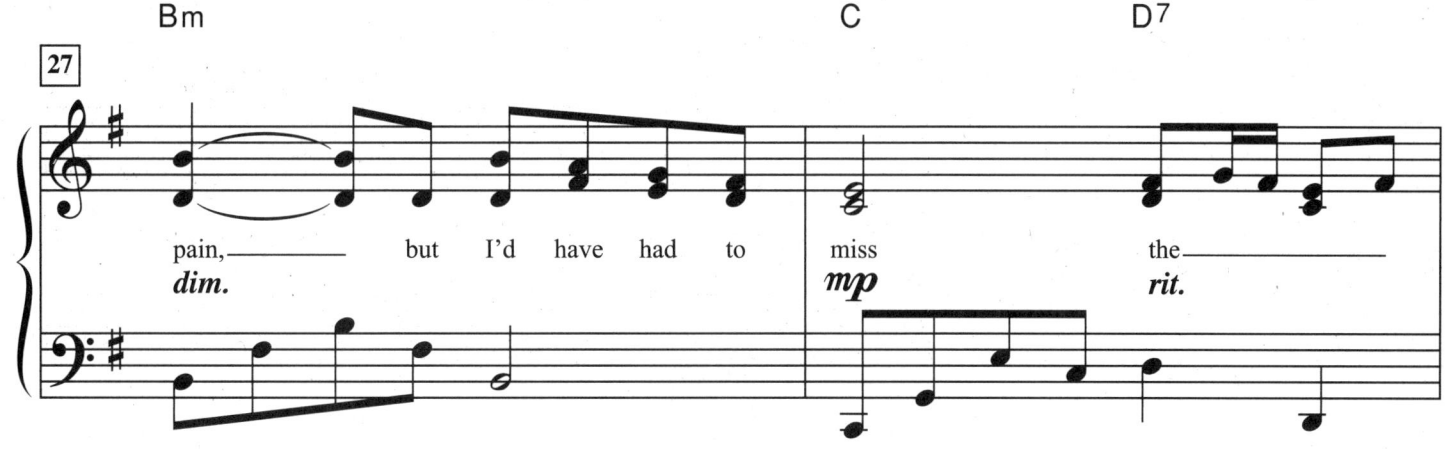

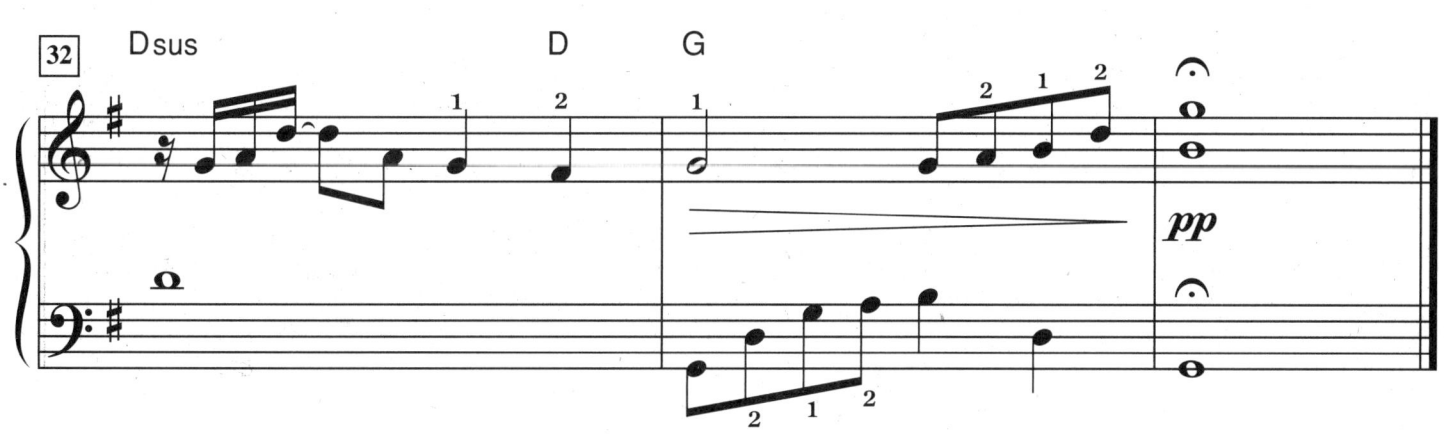

BECAUSE YOU LOVED ME

(Theme from "Up Close and Personal")

Words and Music by Diane Warren
Arranged by Dan Coates

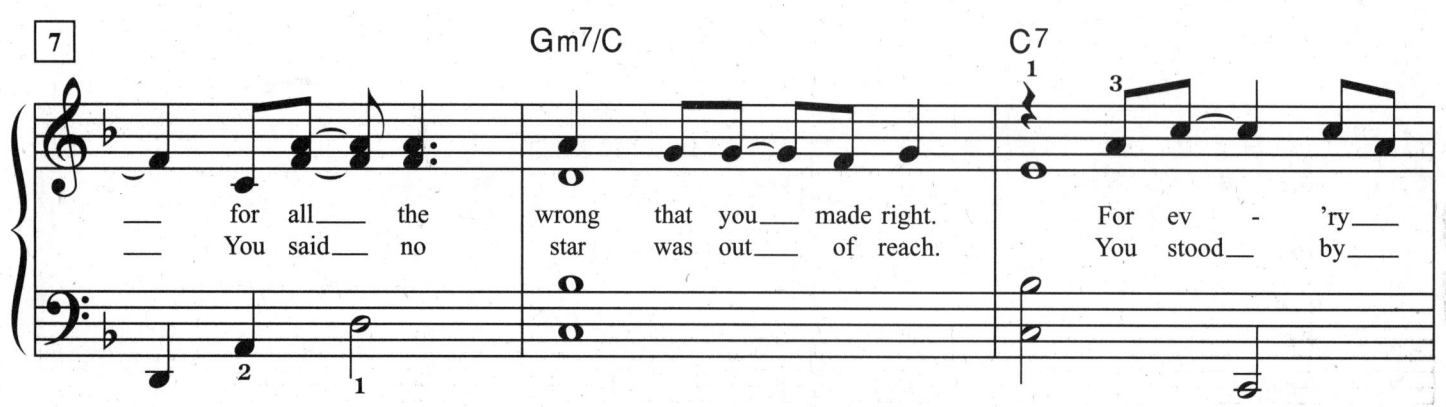

© 1996 REALSONGS (ASCAP) and TOUCHSTONE PICTURES SONGS & MUSIC, INC. (ASCAP)
All Rights Reserved

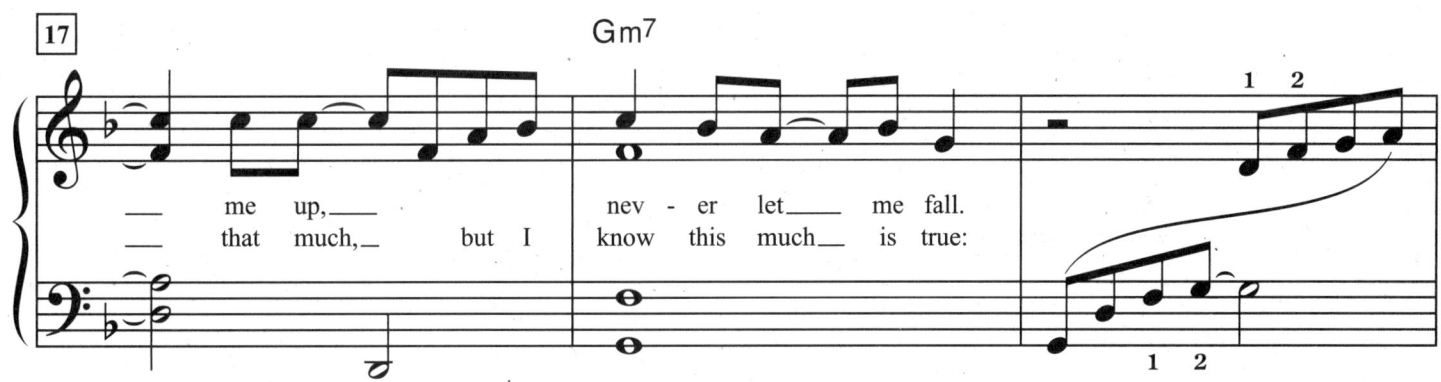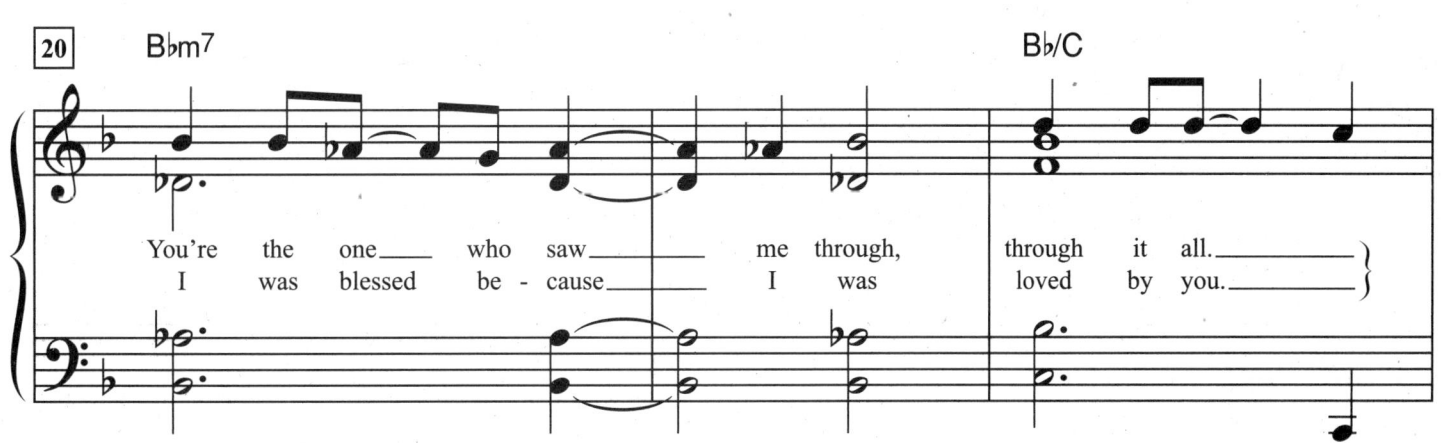

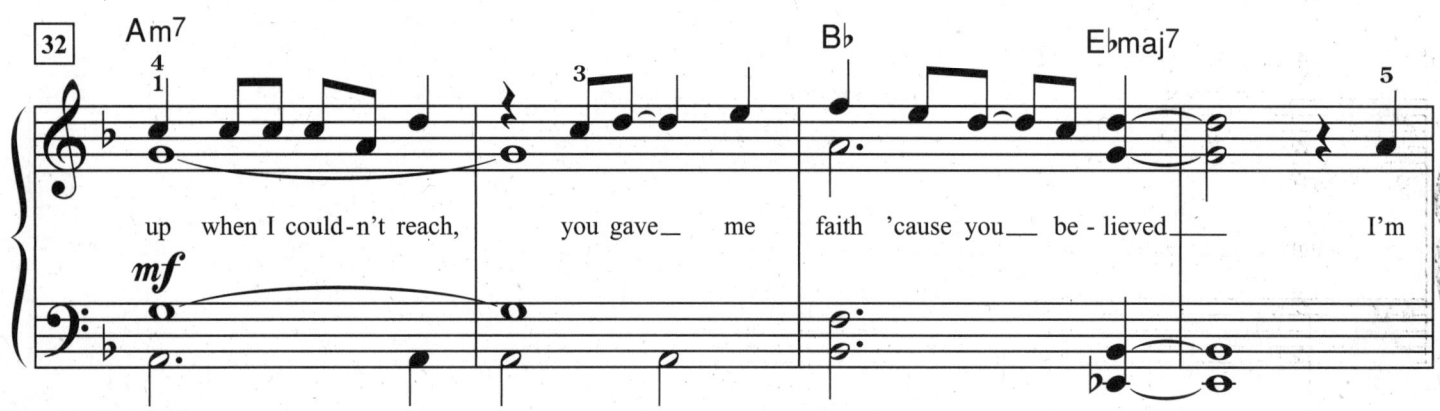

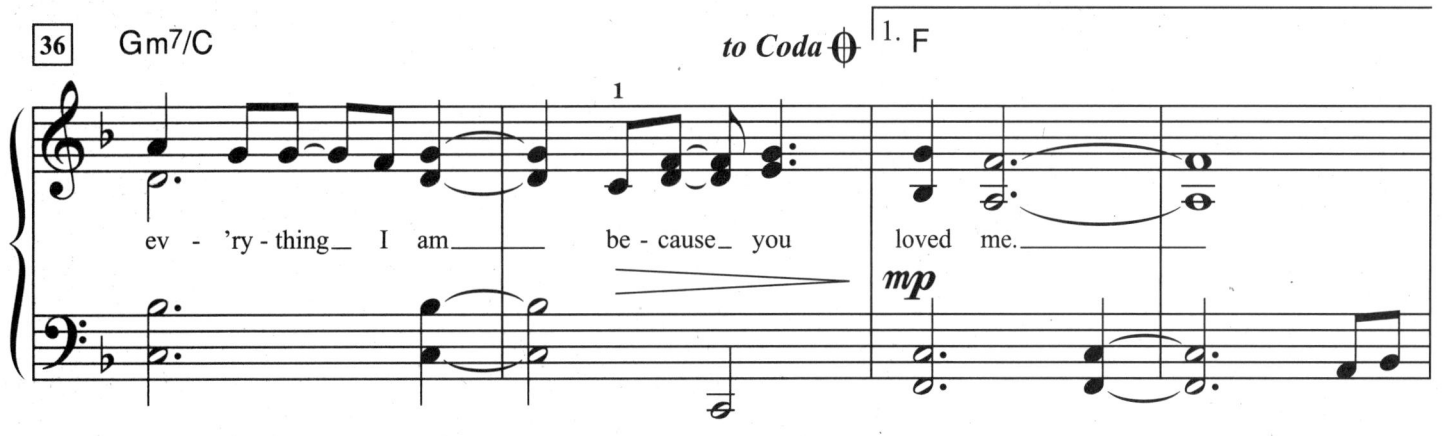
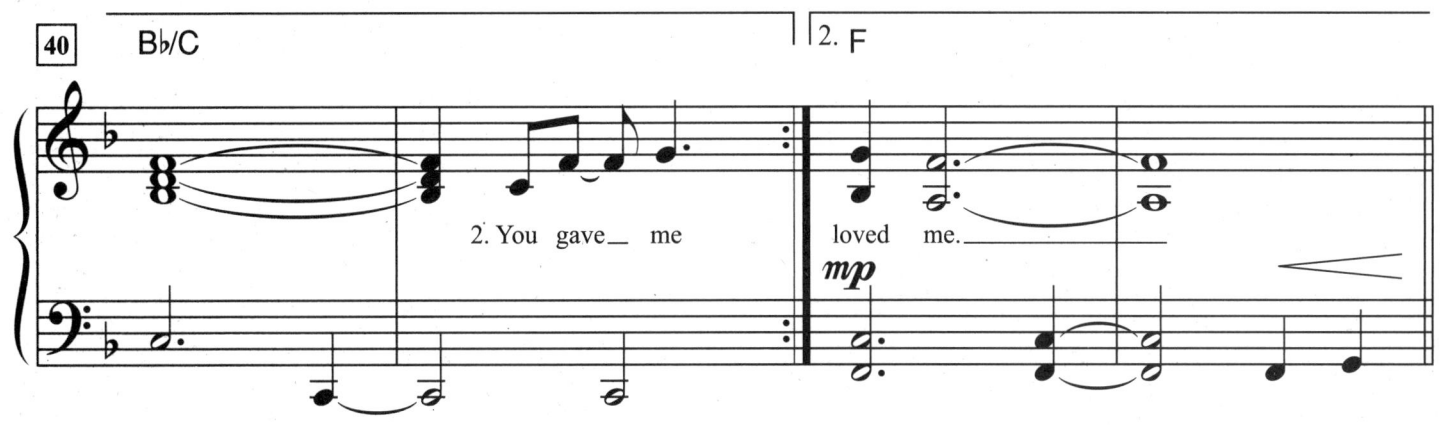
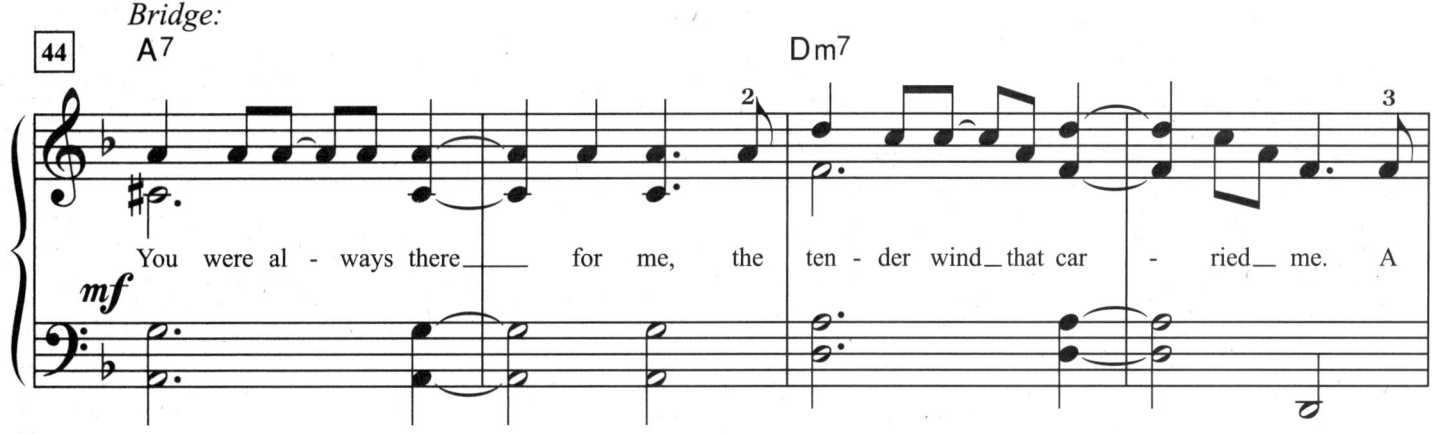

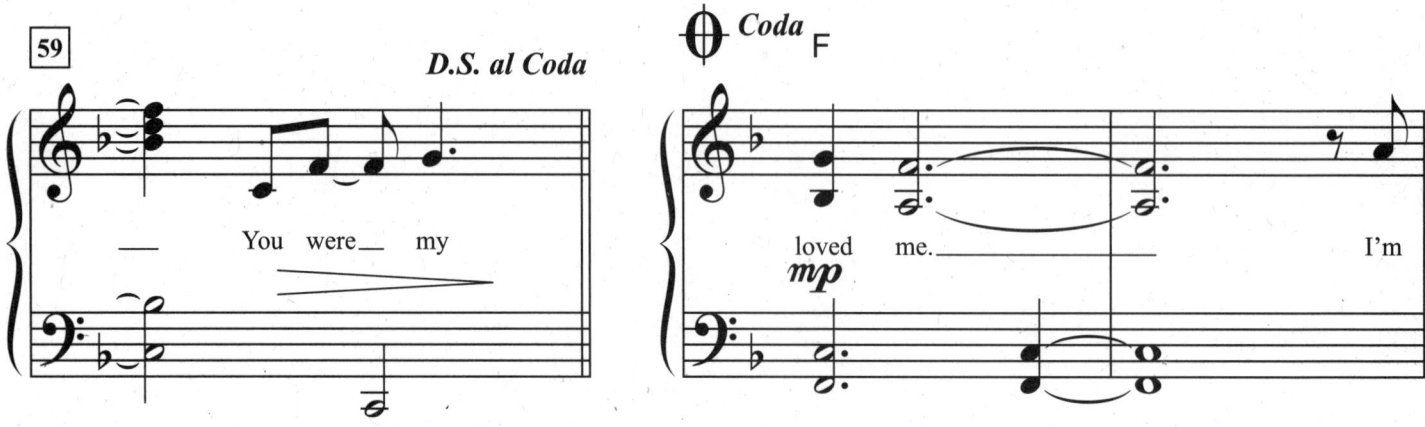

FROM A DISTANCE

Lyrics and Music by Julie Gold
Arranged by Dan Coates

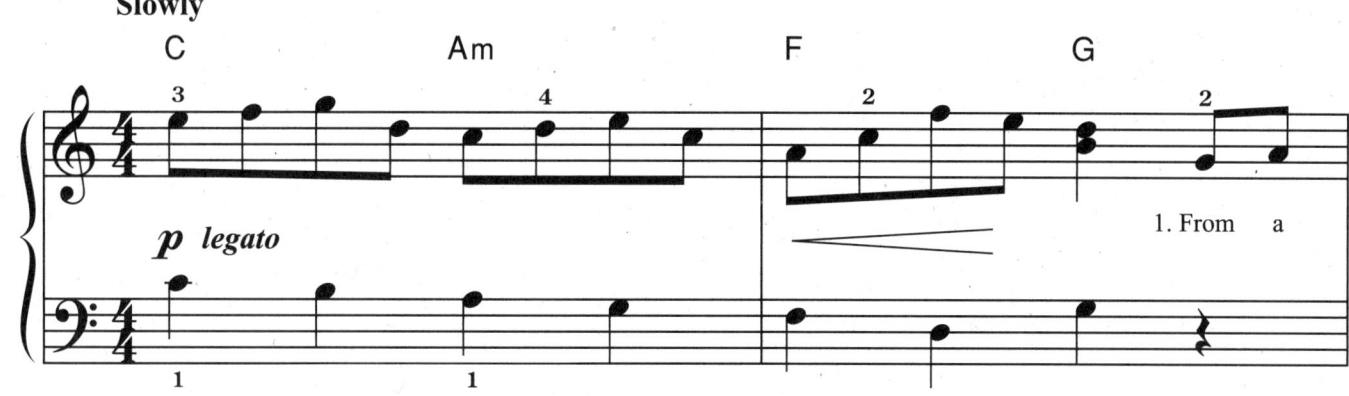

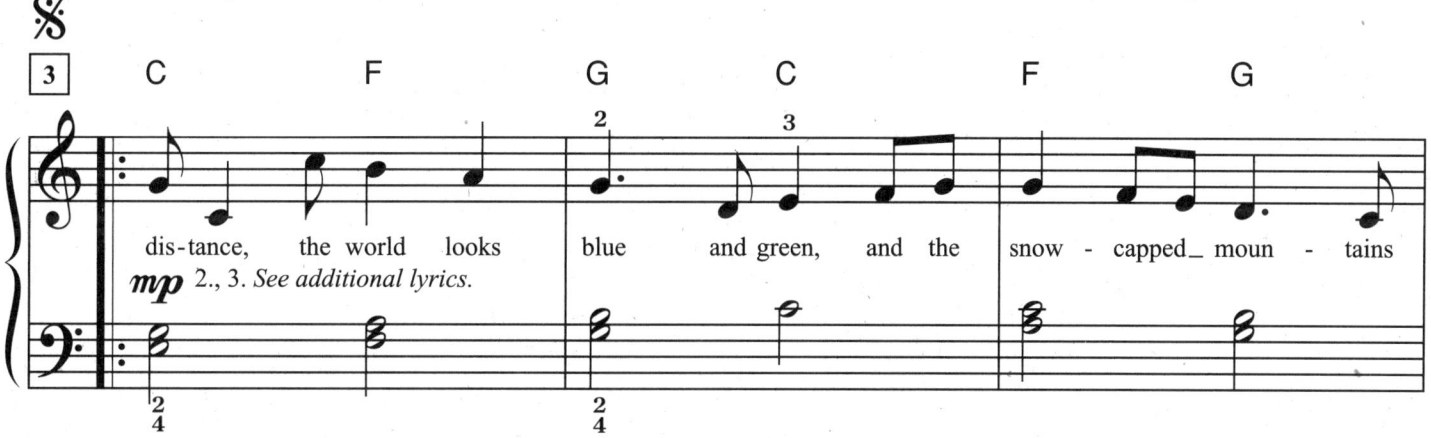

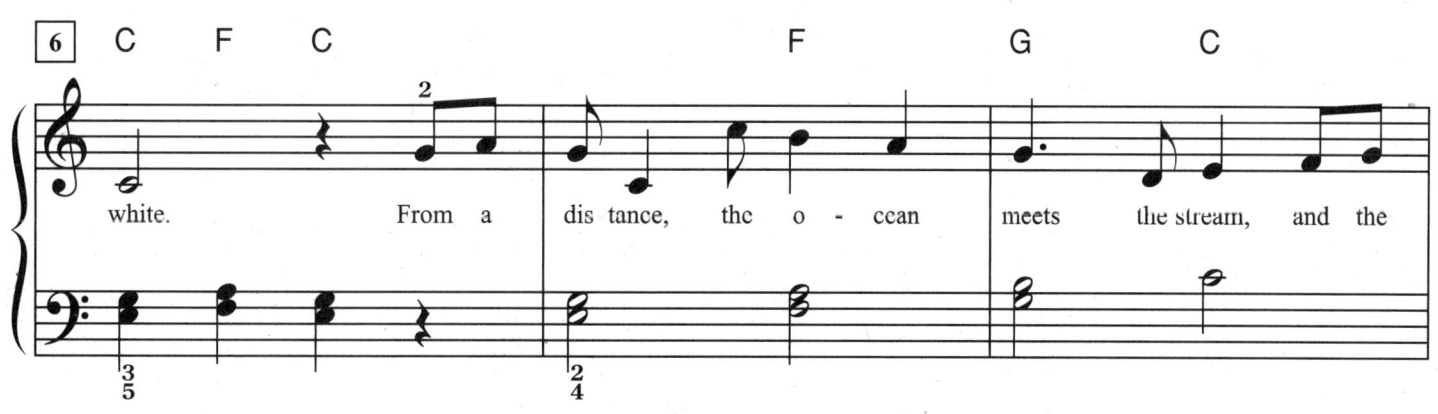

© 1987 WING AND WHEEL MUSIC and JULIE GOLD MUSIC
Worldwide Rights for JULIE GOLD MUSIC Administered by CHERRY RIVER MUSIC CO.
All Rights for WING AND WHEEL MUSIC Administered by IRVING MUSIC, INC.
All Rights Reserved   Used by Permission

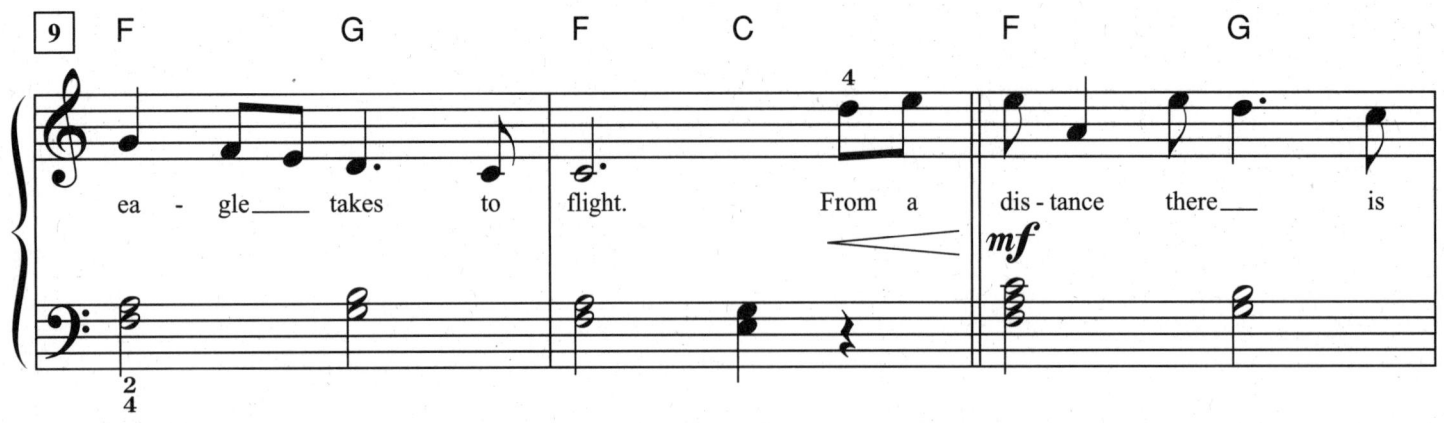
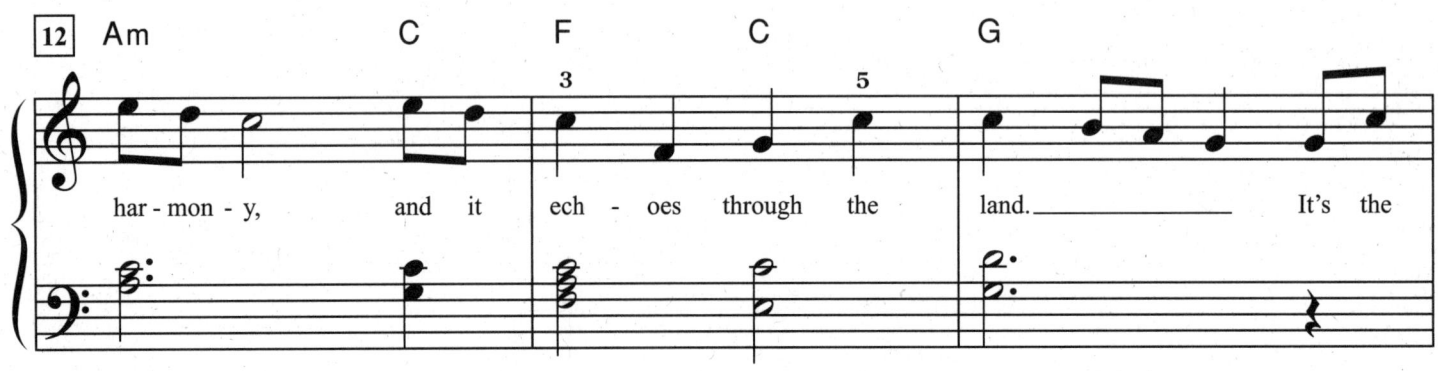
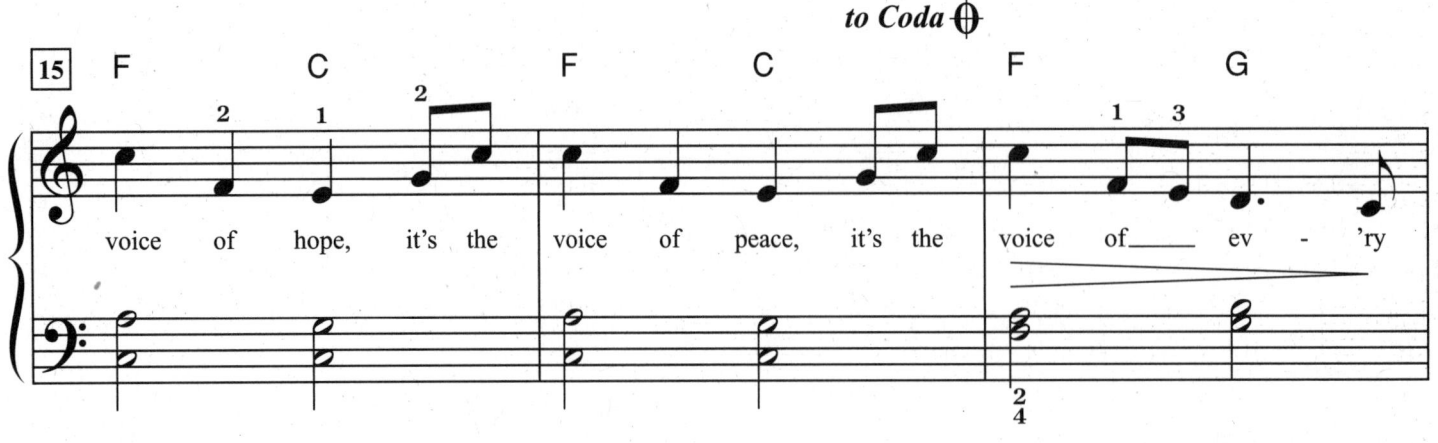

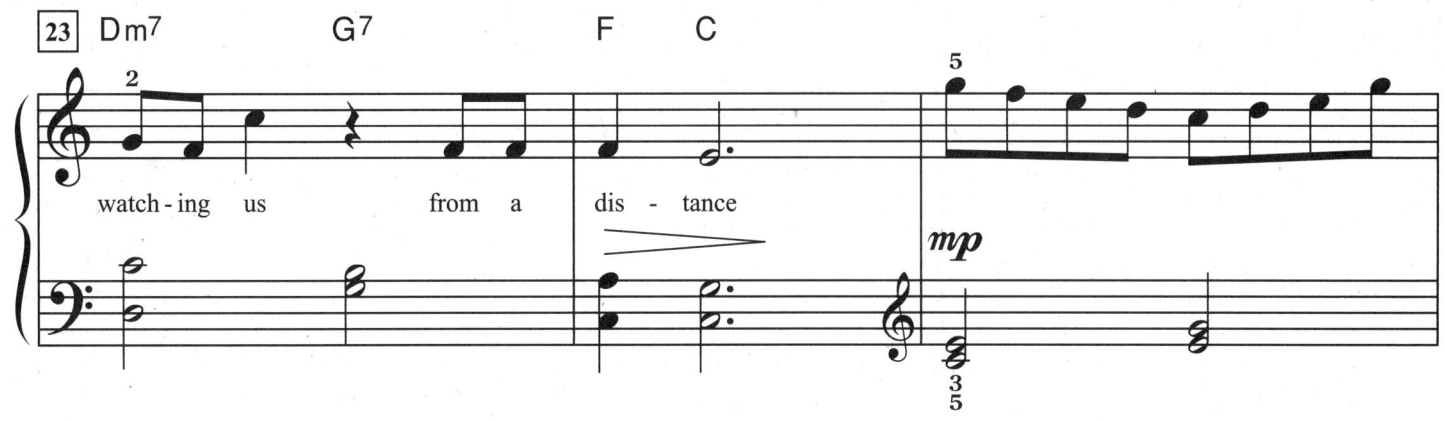
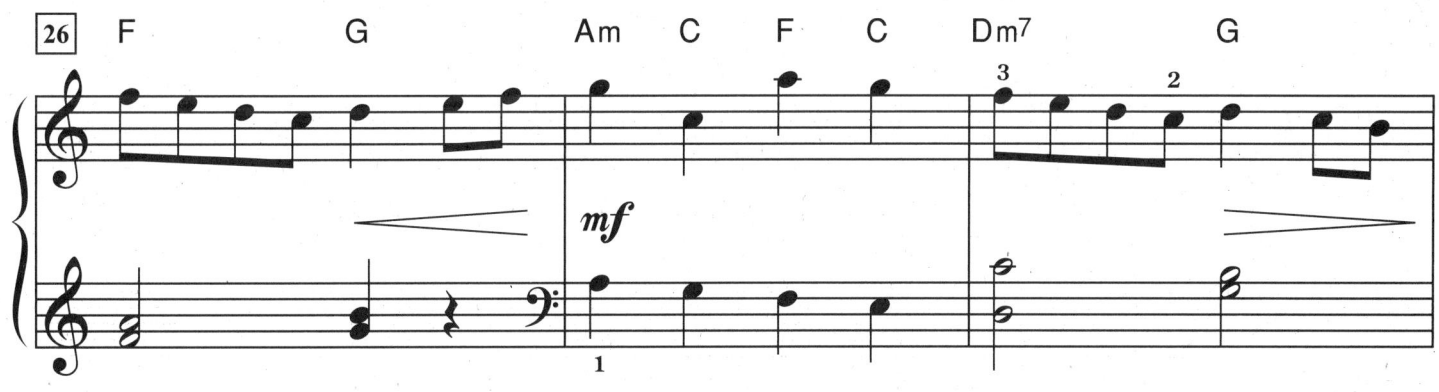
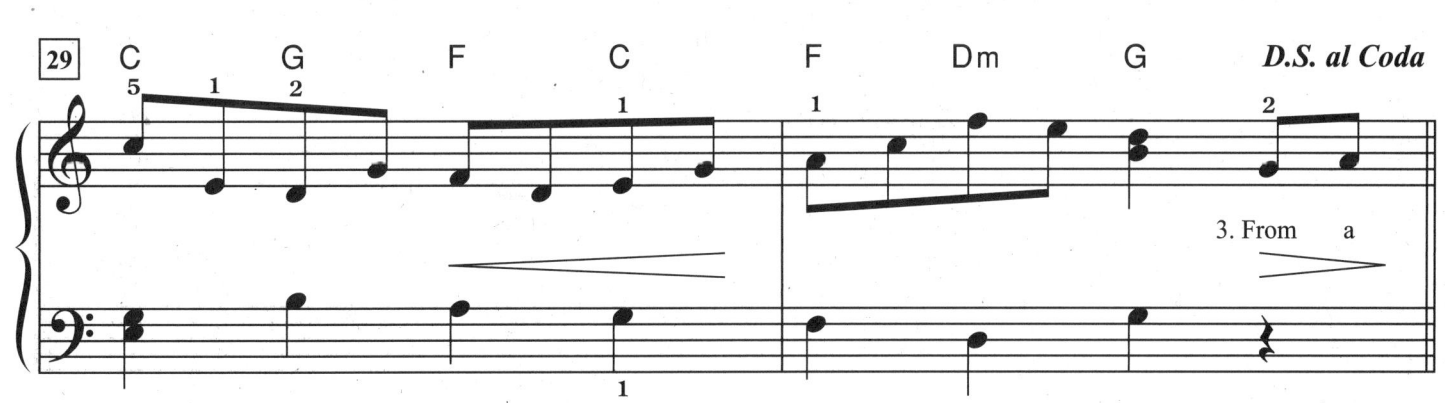

20

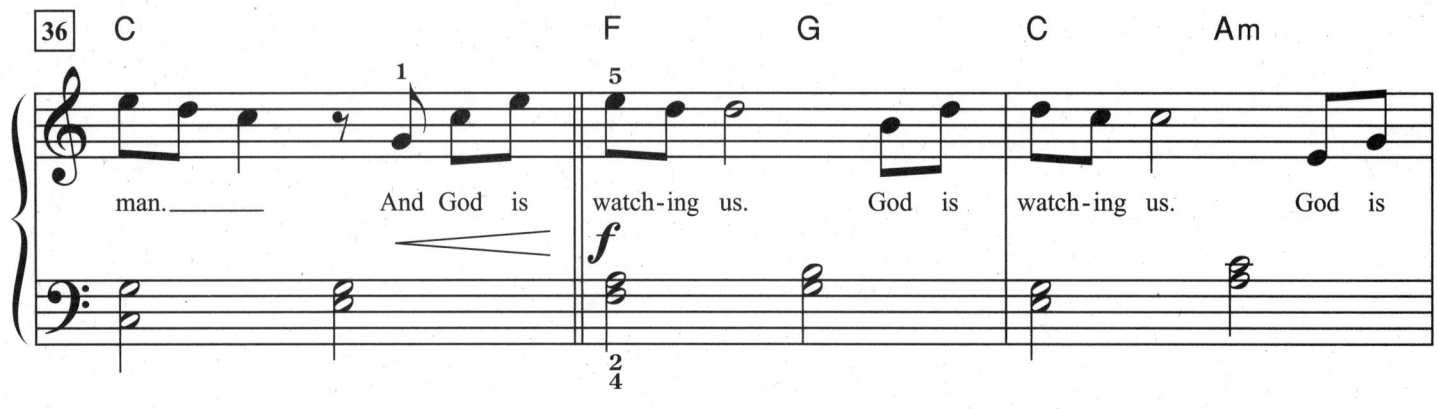

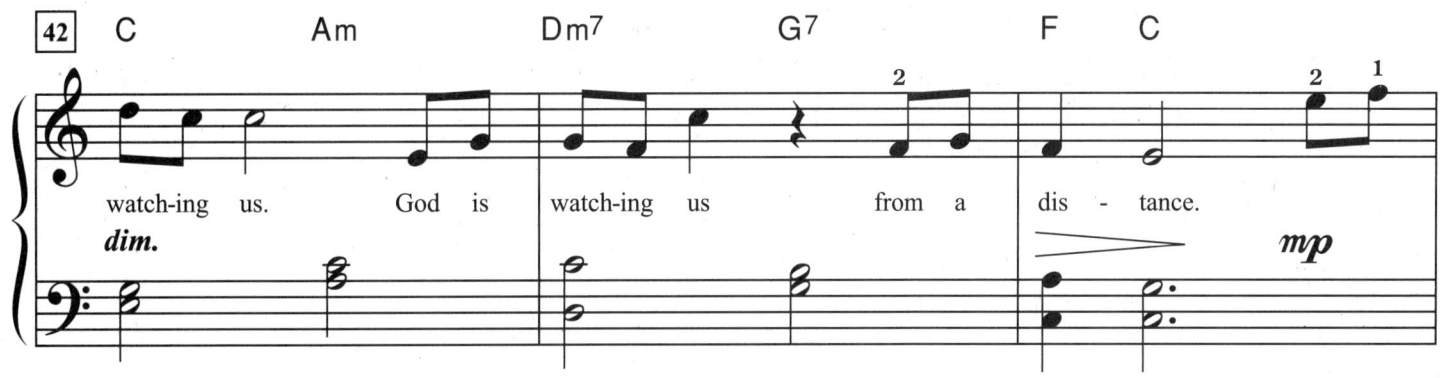

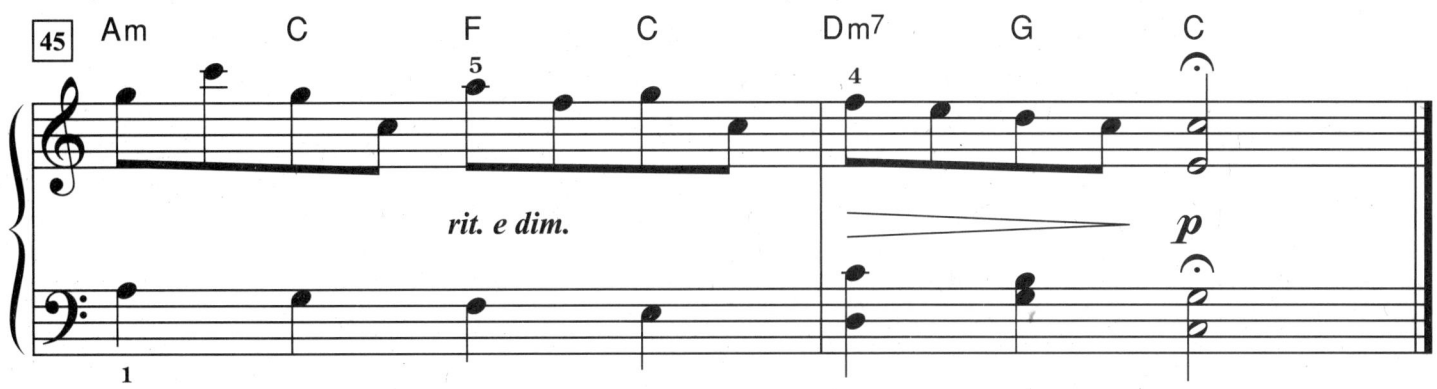

Verse 2:
From a distance, we all have enough
And no one is in need.
There are no guns, no bombs, no disease,
No hungry mouths to feed.
From a distance, we are instruments
Marching in a common band;
Playing songs of hope, playing songs of peace,
They're the songs of every man.

Verse 3:
From a distance, you look like my friend
Even though we are at war.
From a distance, I just can't comprehend
What all this fighting is for.
From a distance, there is harmony
And it echoes through the land.
It's the hope of hopes. It's the love of loves.
It's the heart of every man.

THE GREATEST LOVE OF ALL

Words by Linda Creed
Music by Michael Masser
Arranged by Dan Coates

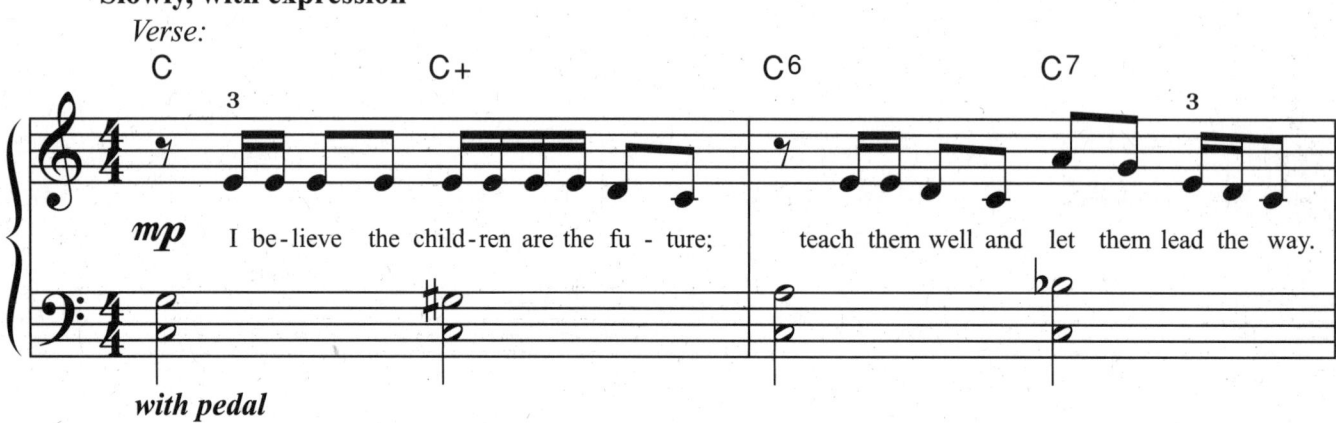

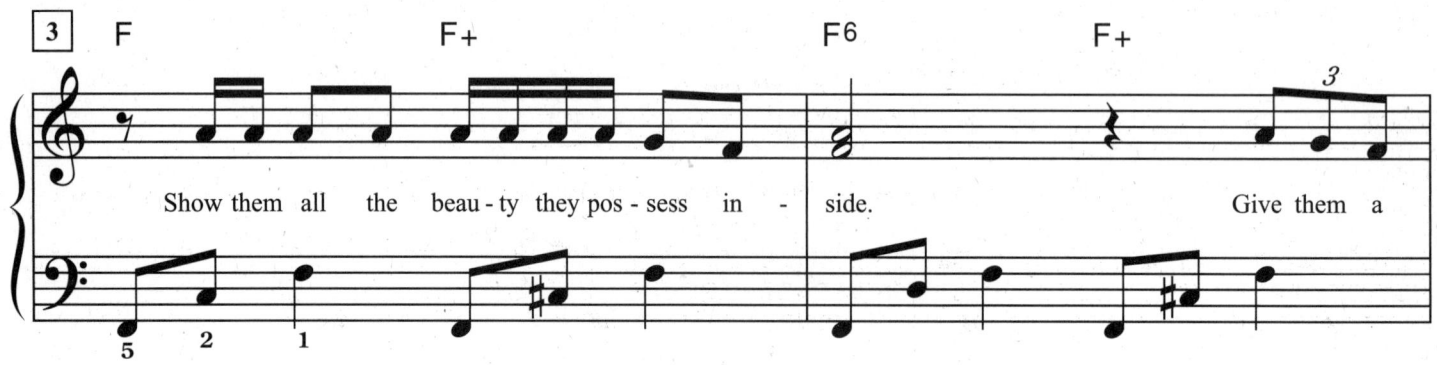

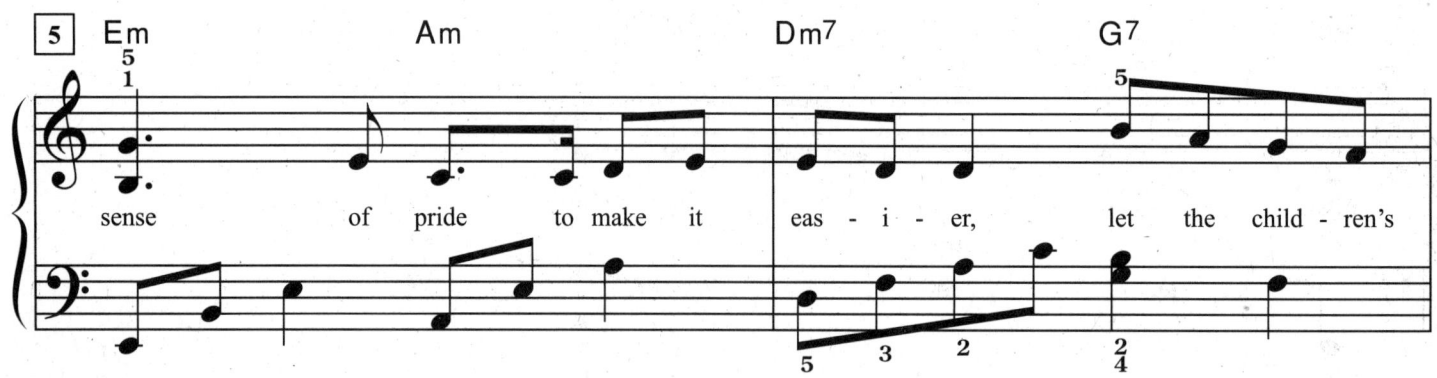

© 1977 (Renewed) EMI GOLD HORIZON MUSIC CORP. and EMI GOLDEN TORCH MUSIC CORP.
Exclusive Print Rights Administered by ALFRED MUSIC PUBLISHING CO., INC.
All Rights Reserved

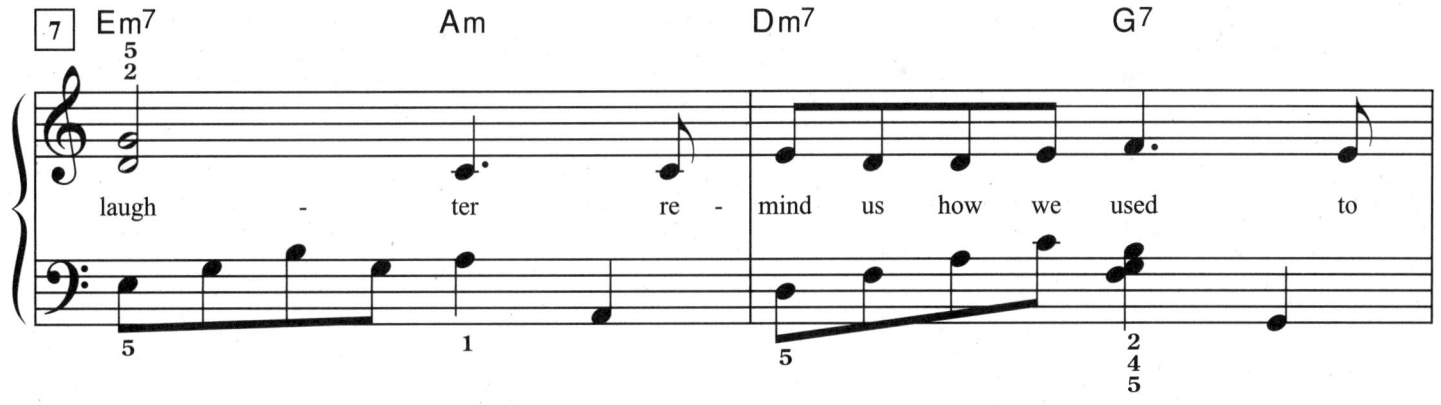
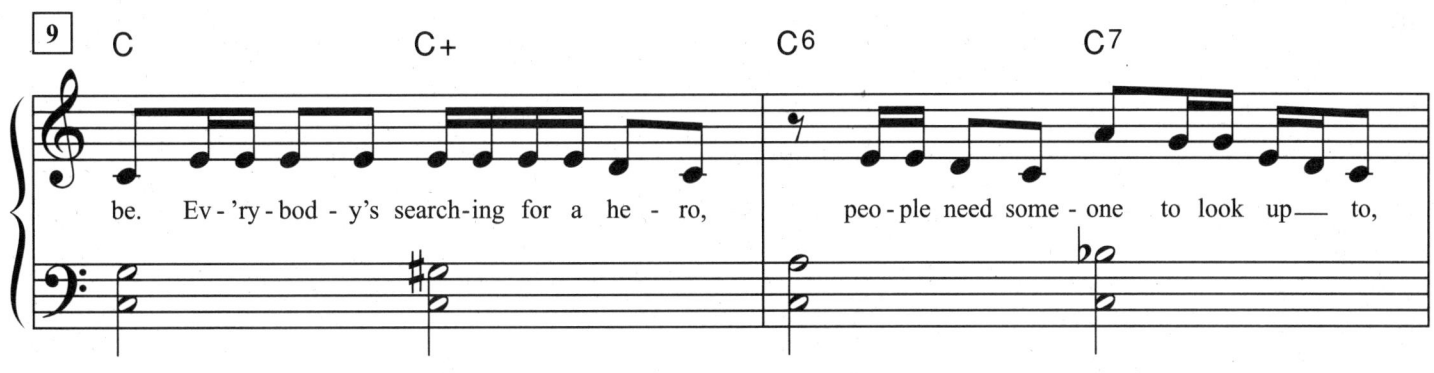

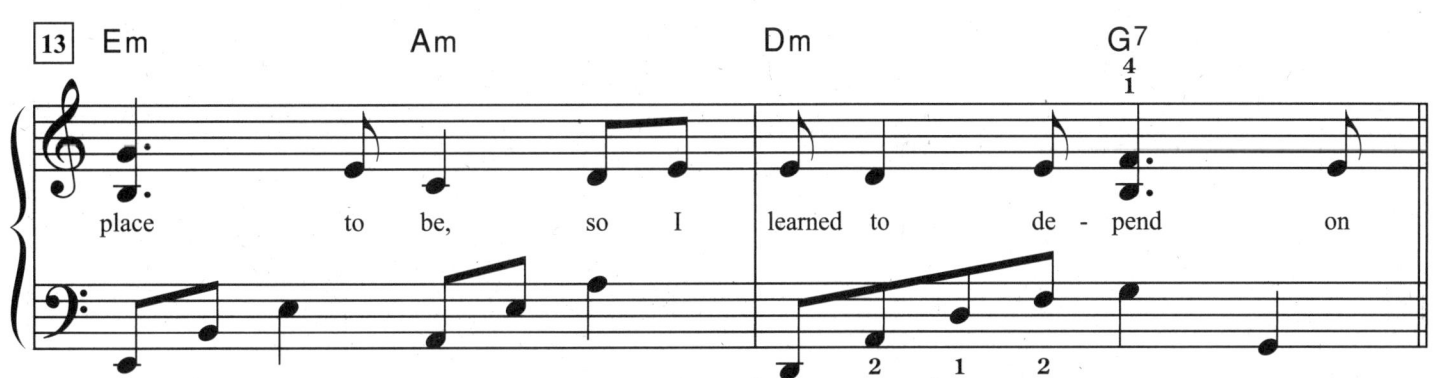

24

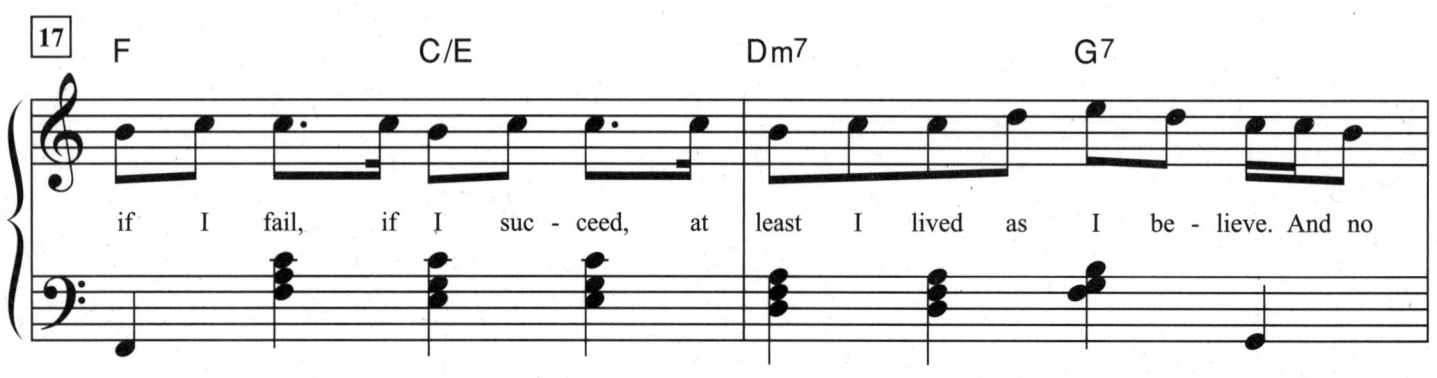

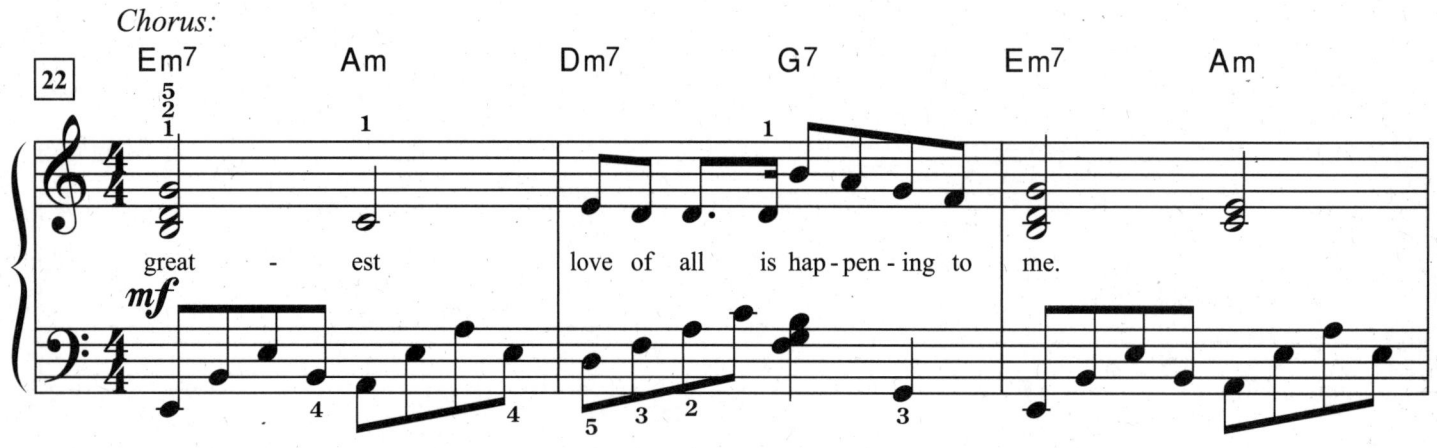

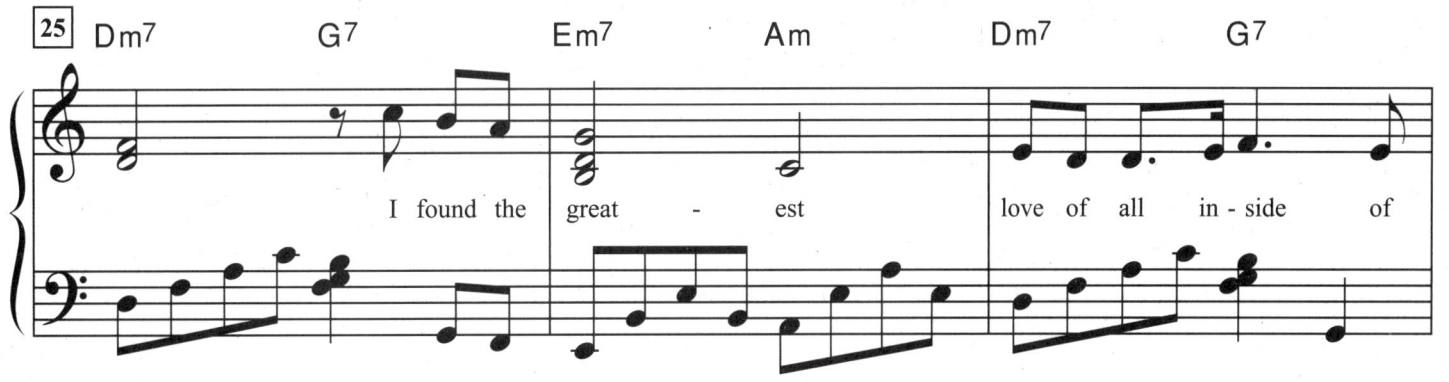

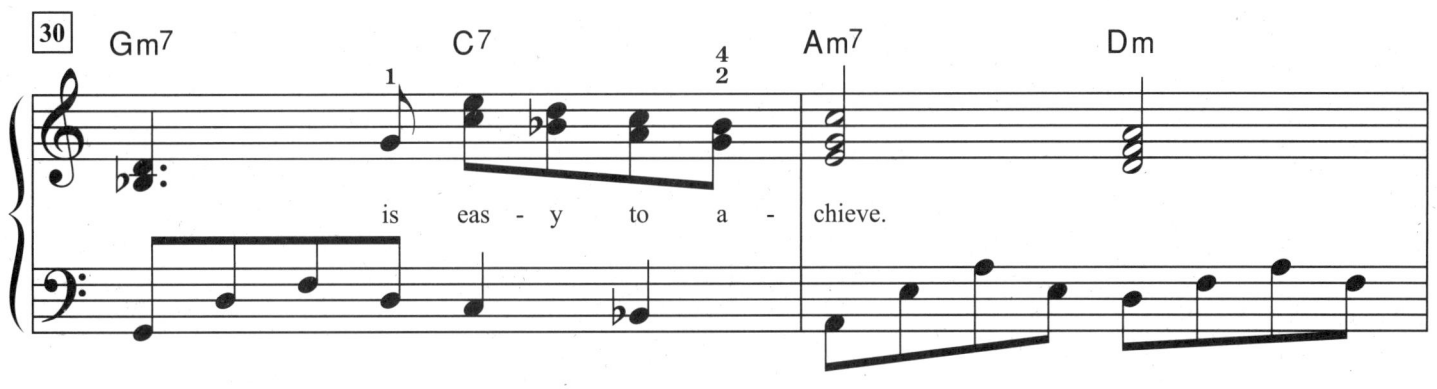
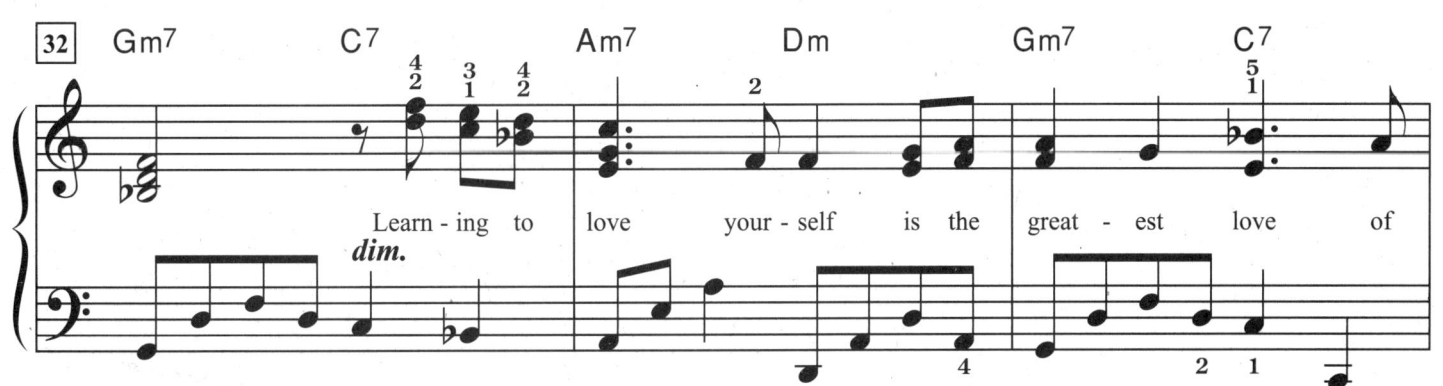

26

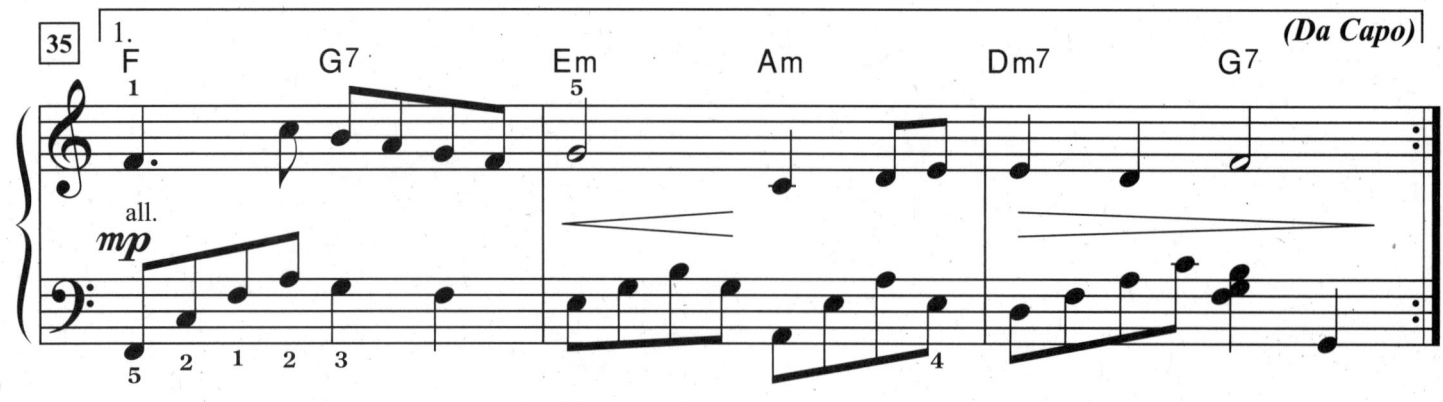
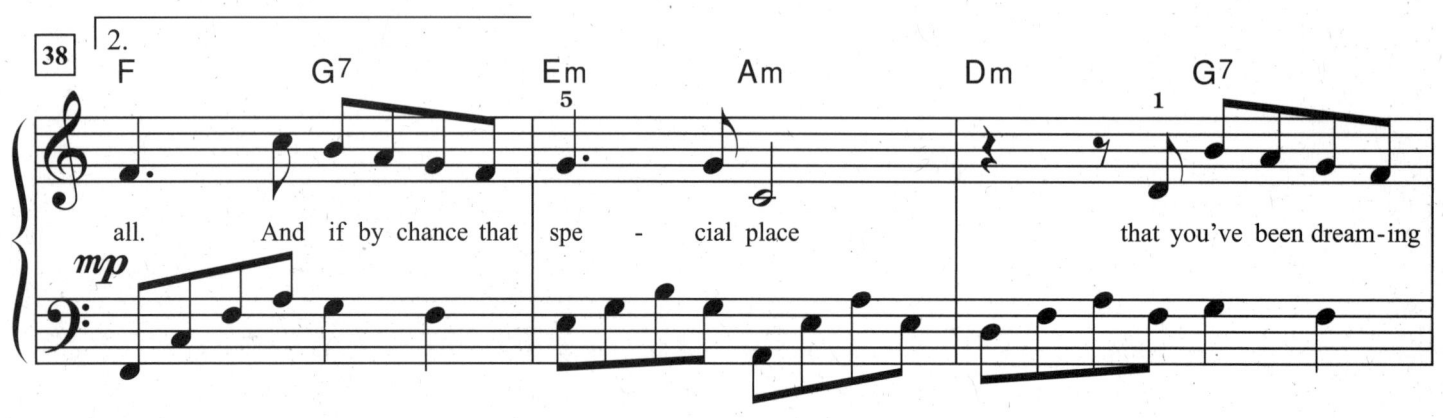
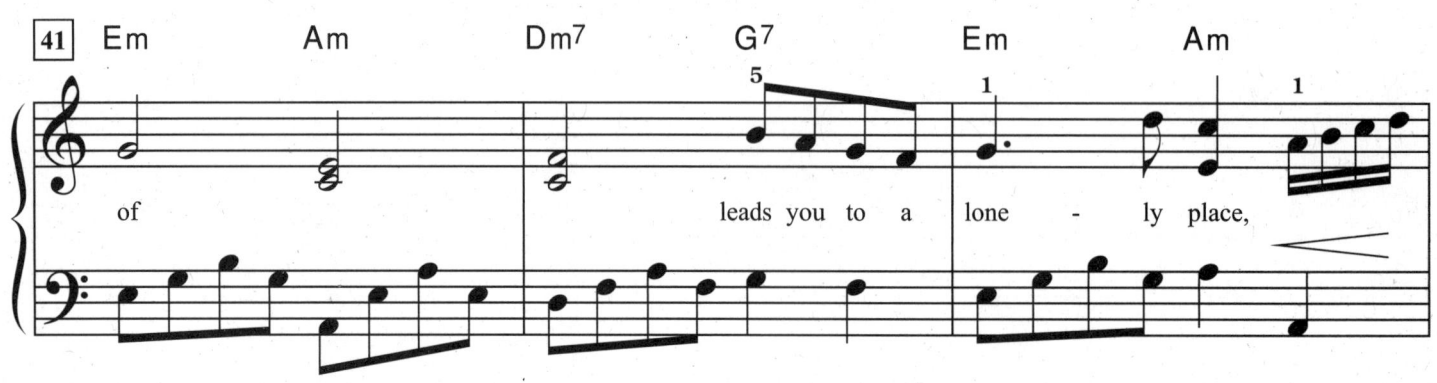
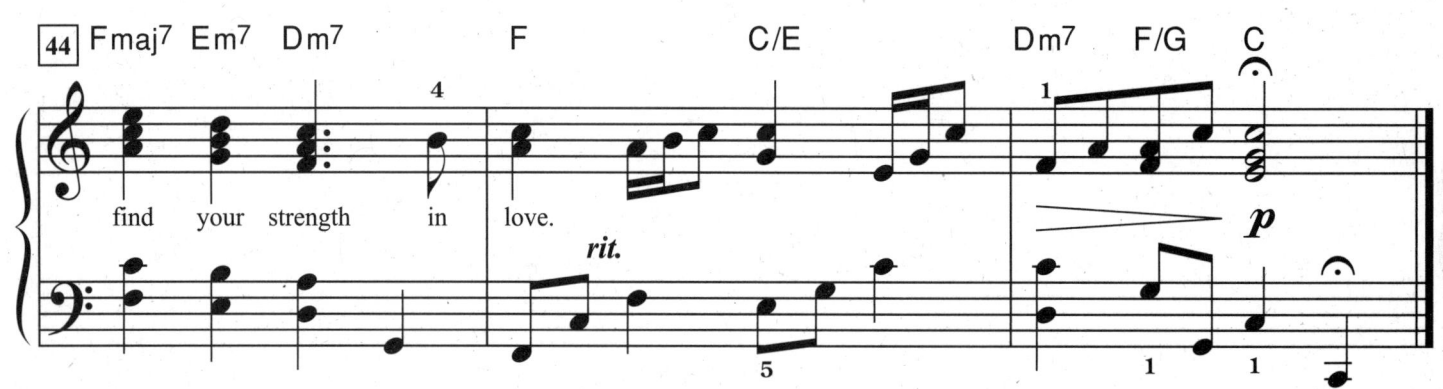

HERO

HEAL THE WORLD

Written and Composed by Michael Jackson
Arranged by Dan Coates

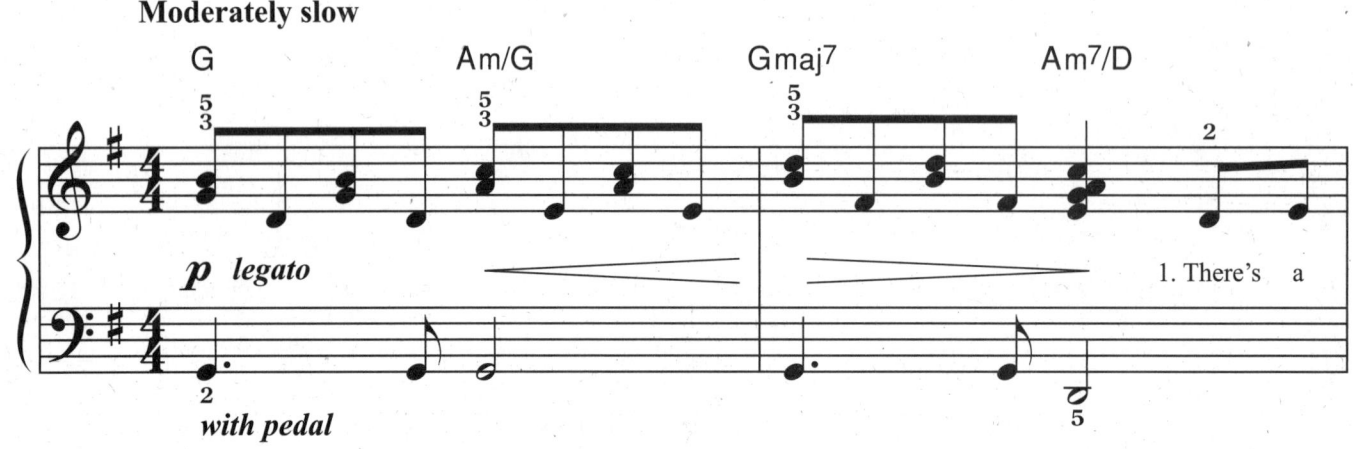
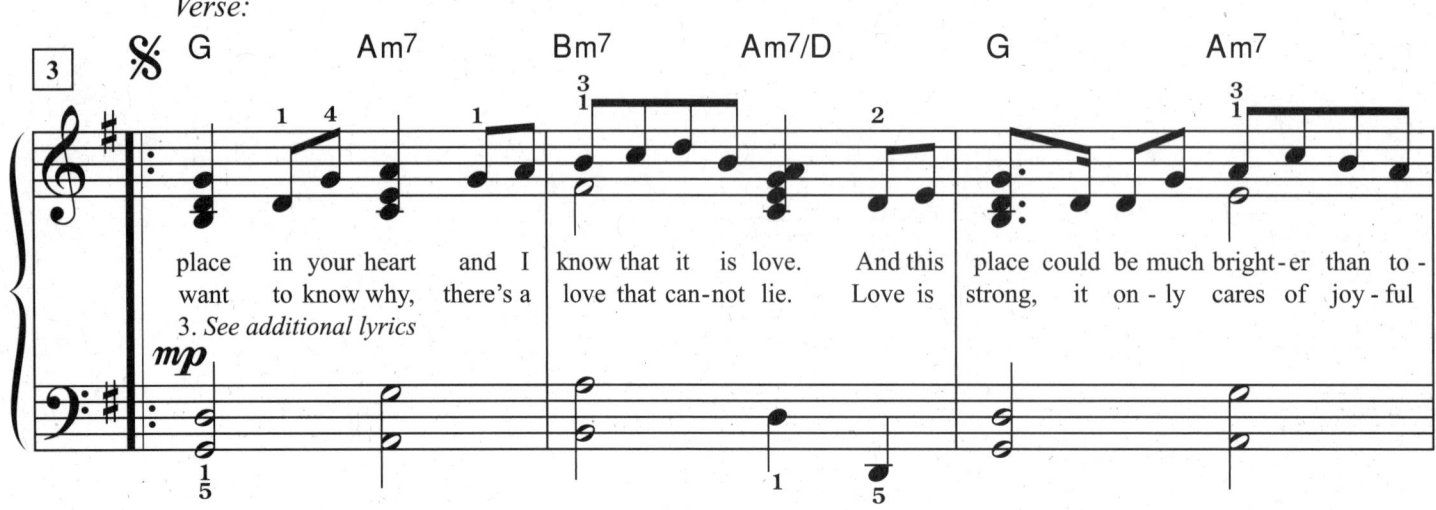
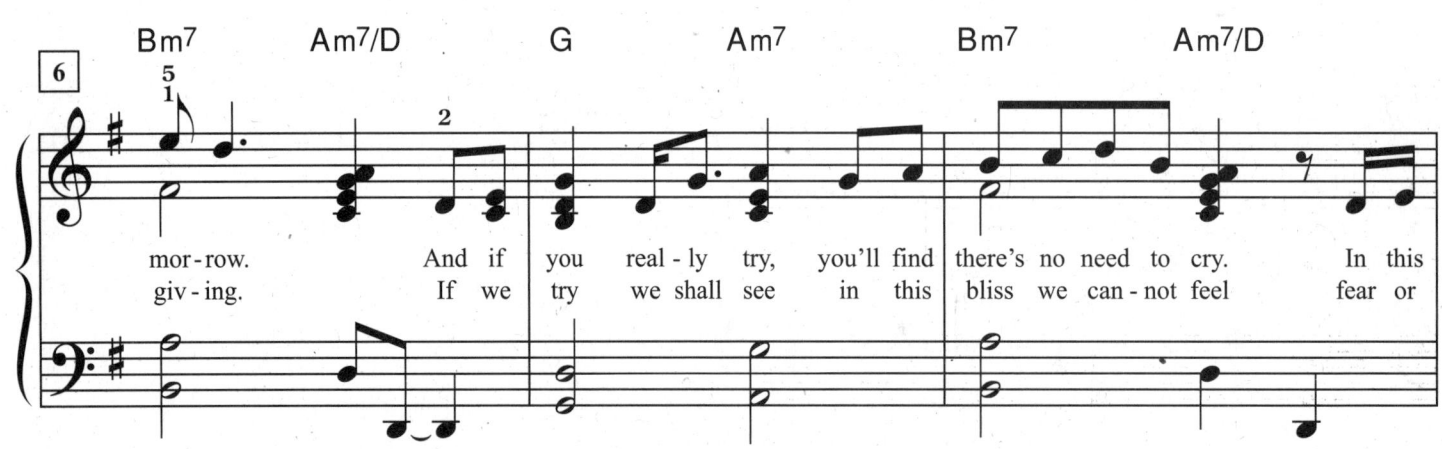

© 1991 MIJAC MUSIC (BMI)
All Rights Administered by WARNER-TAMERLANE PUBLISHING CORP.
All Rights Reserved

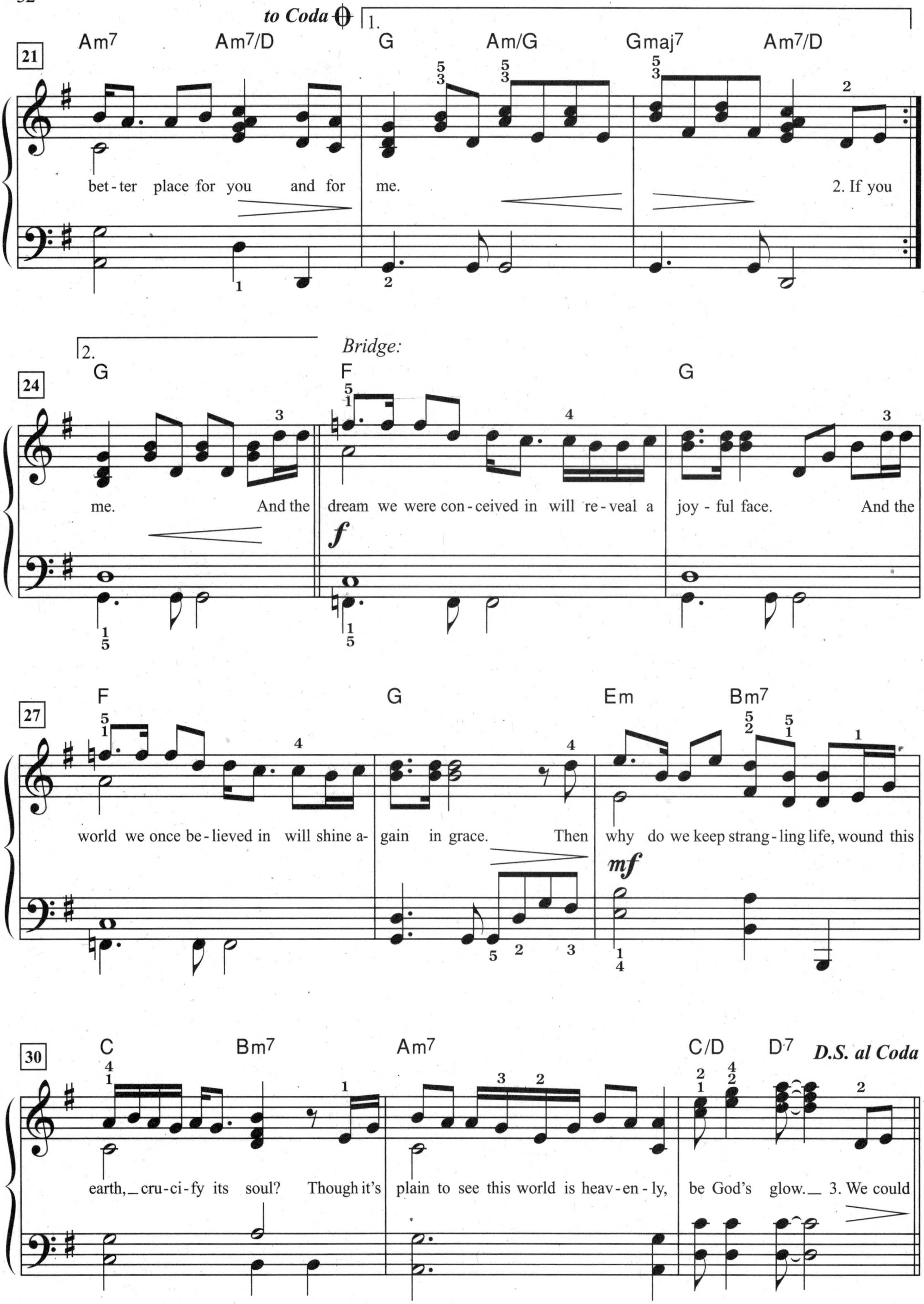
to Coda
1.
21
Am7 Am7/D G Am/G Gmaj7 Am7/D
bet - ter place for you and for me. 2. If you
2.
Bridge:
24
G F G
me. And the dream we were con - ceived in will re - veal a joy - ful face. And the
f
27
F G Em Bm7
world we once be - lieved in will shine a- gain in grace. Then why do we keep strang - ling life, wound this
mf
30
C Bm7 Am7 C/D D7 D.S. al Coda
earth, cru - ci - fy its soul? Though it's plain to see this world is heav - en - ly, be God's glow. 3. We could

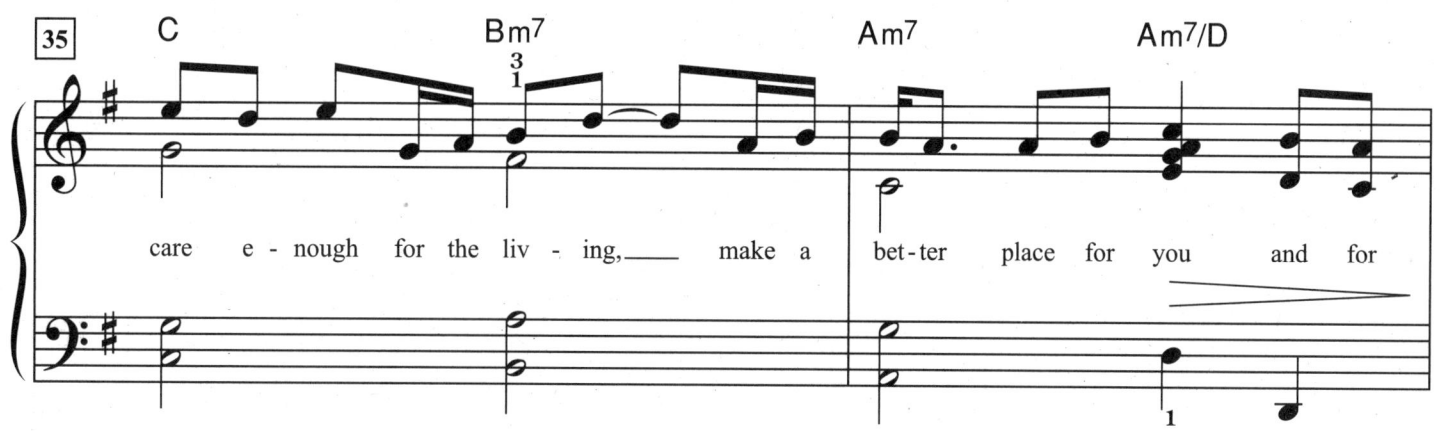

Verse 3:
We could fly so high,
Let our spirits never die.
In my heart, I feel you are all my brothers.
Create a world with no fear,
Together we cry happy tears.
See the nation turn their swords into plowshares.
We could really get there,
If you cared enough for the living.
Make a little space
To make a better place.
(To Chorus:)

(YOUR LOVE IS LIFTING ME) HIGHER AND HIGHER

Words and Music by
Gary Jackson, Carl Smith and Raynard Miner
Arranged by Dan Coates

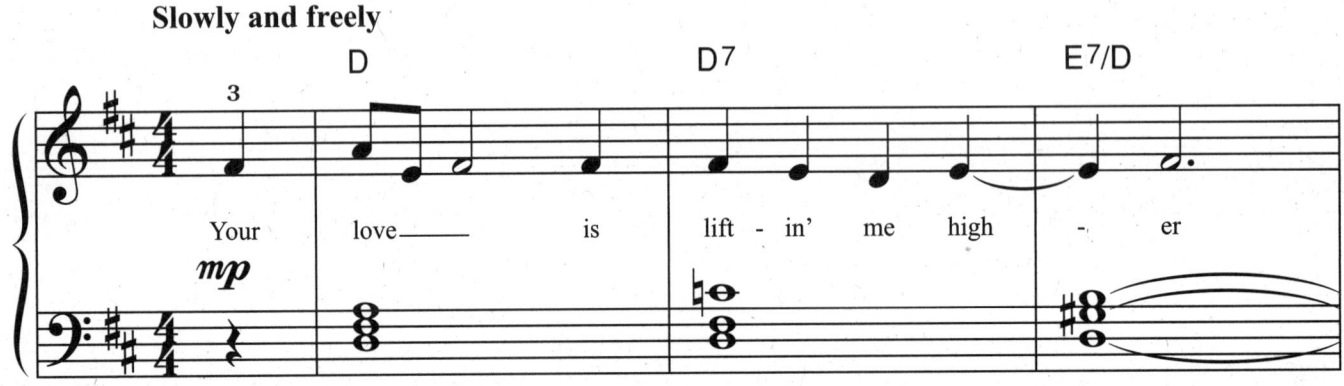
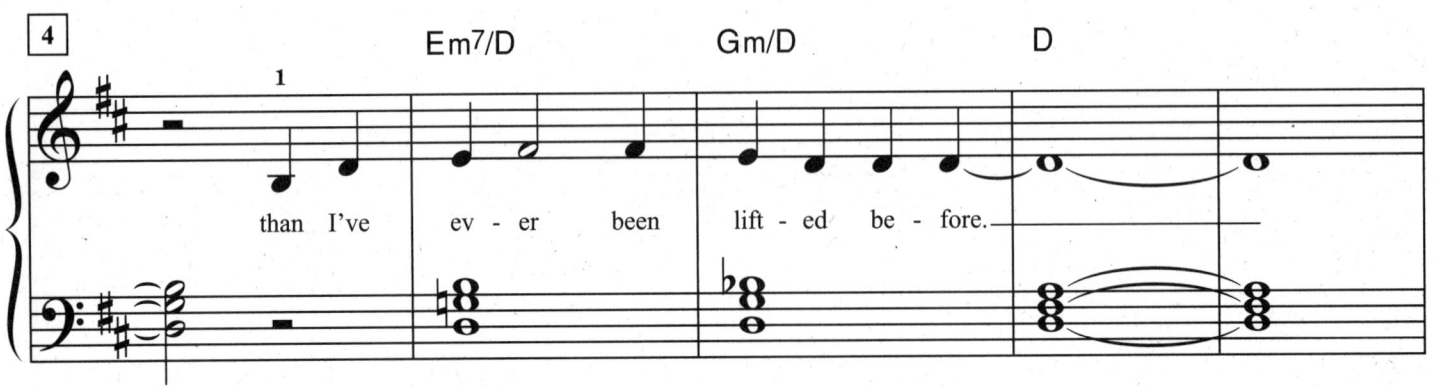
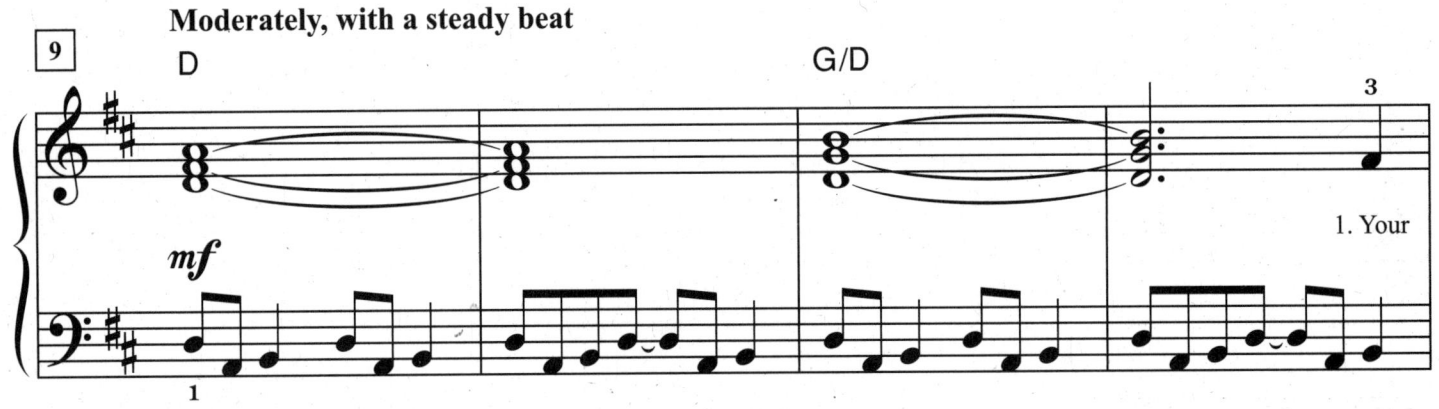

© 1967 (Renewed) UNICHAPPELL MUSIC INC., MIJAC MUSIC, WARNER-TAMERLANE PUBLISHING CORP. and CHEVIS MUSIC, INC.
All Rights on behalf of itself, MIJAC MUSIC and UNICHAPPELL MUSIC INC. Administered by WARNER-TAMERLANE PUBLISHING CORP.
All Rights Reserved

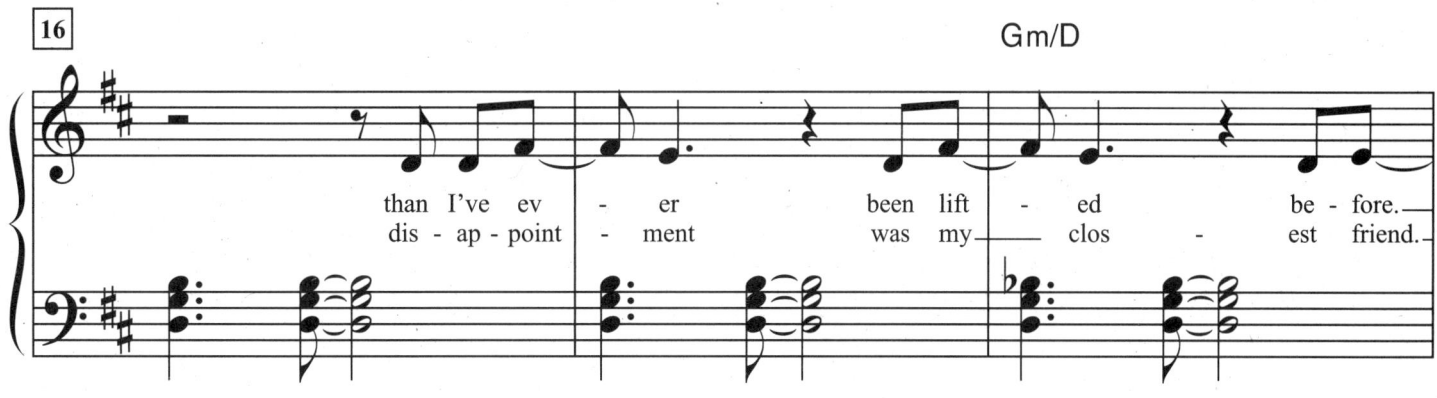

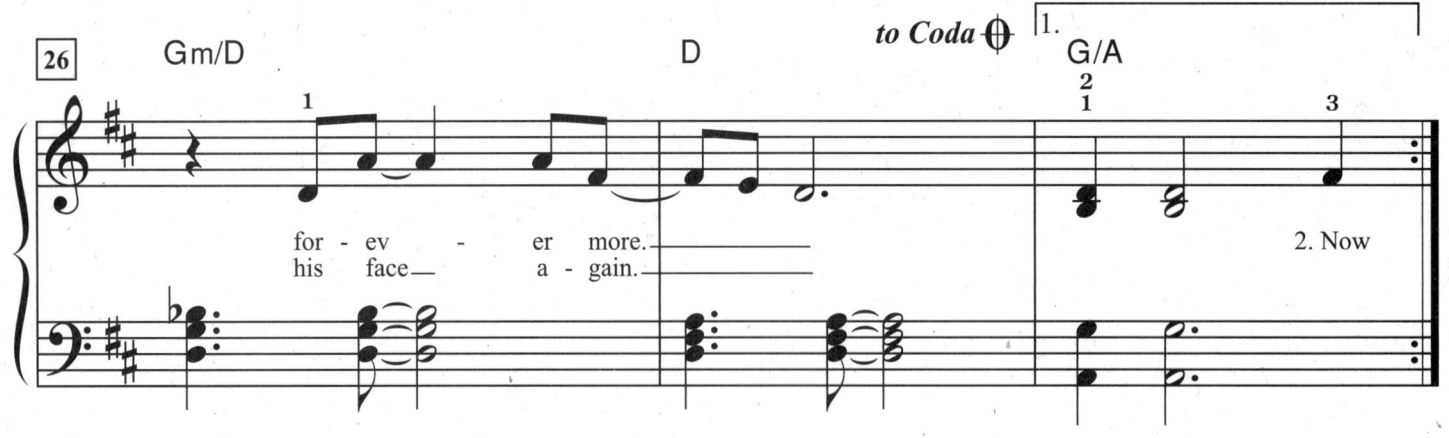
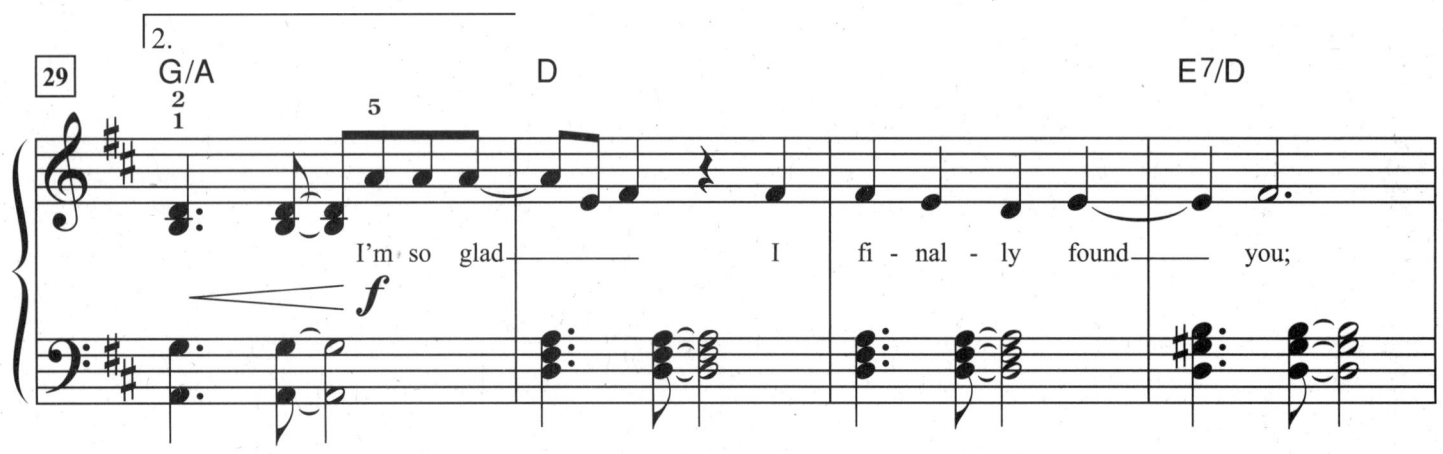
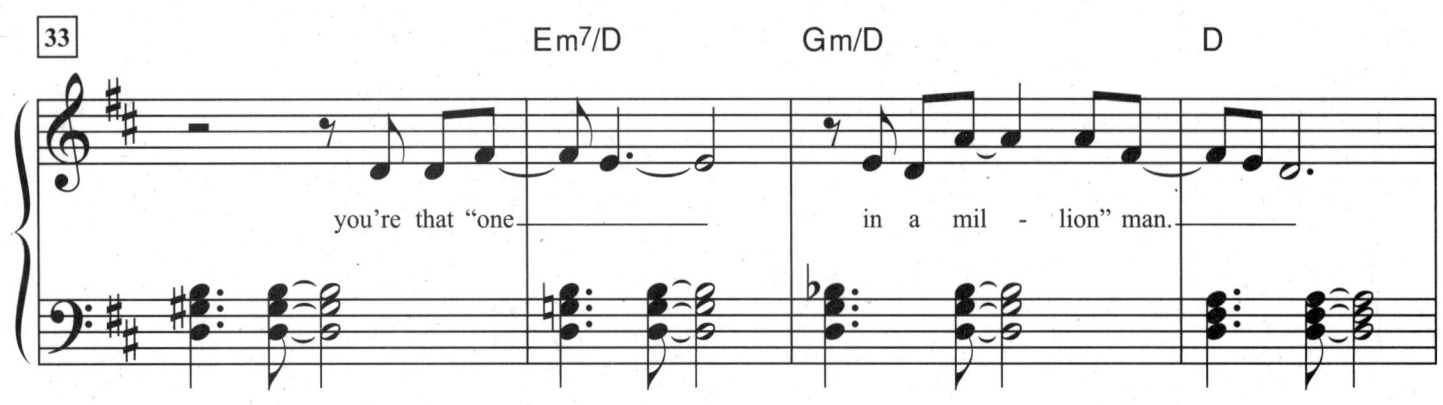

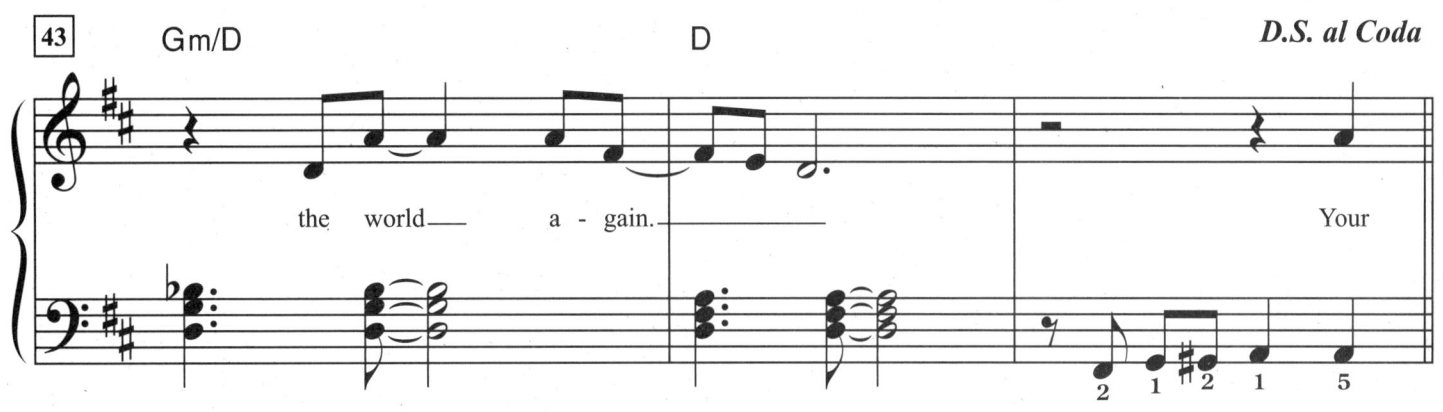
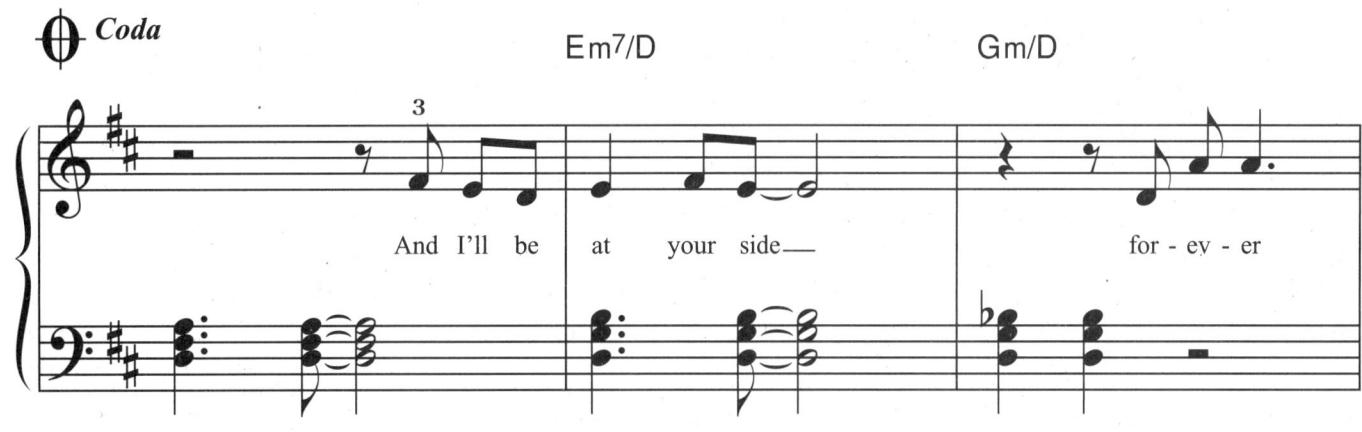

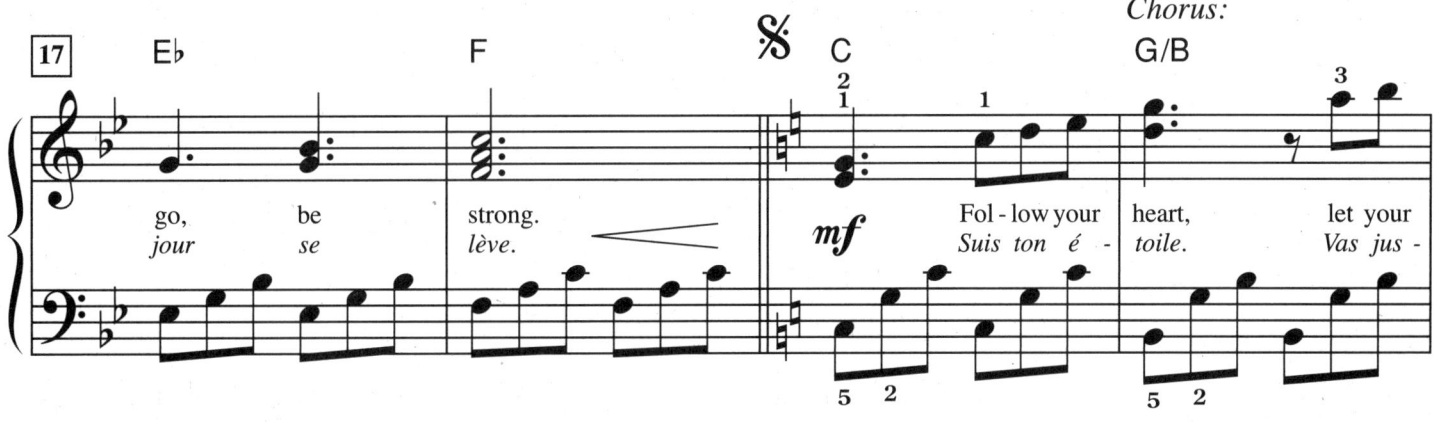

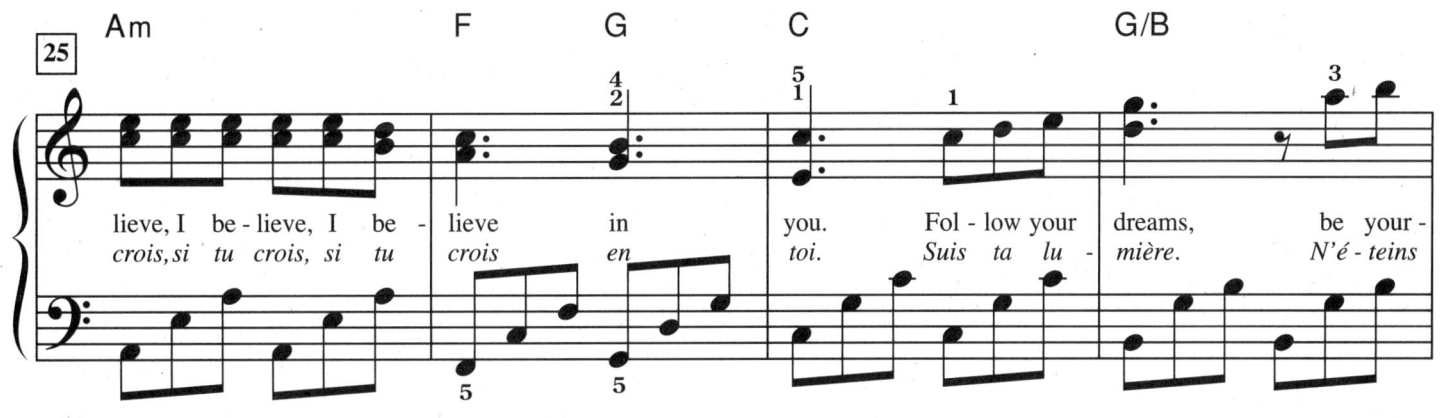

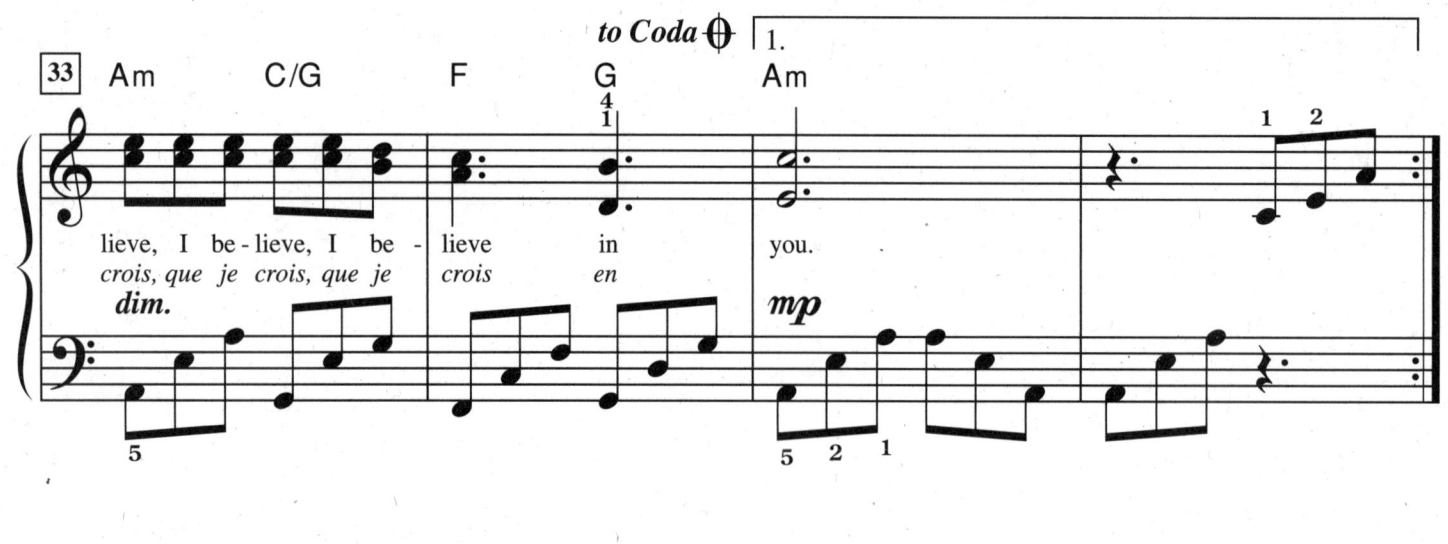
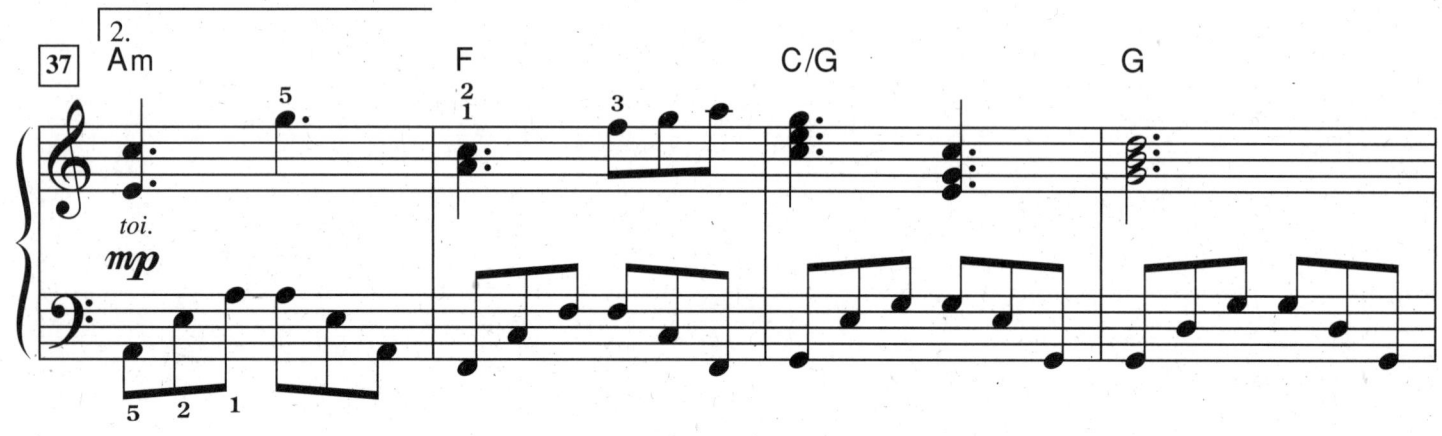
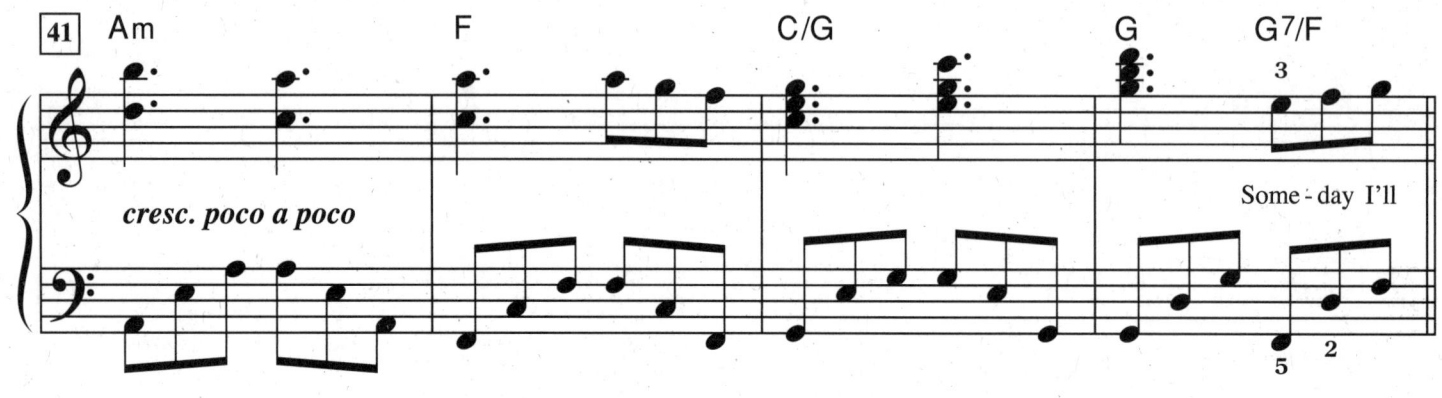

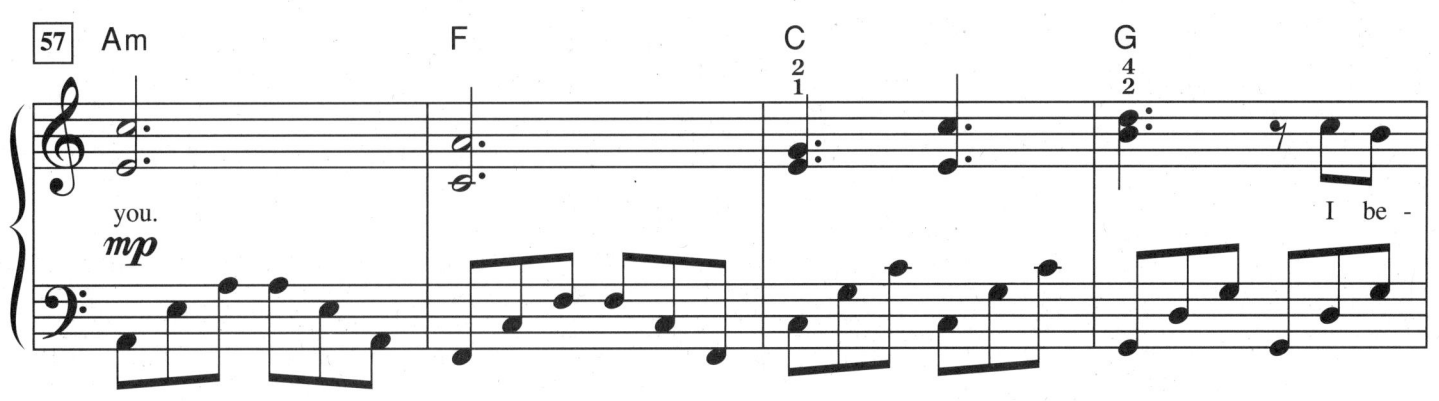
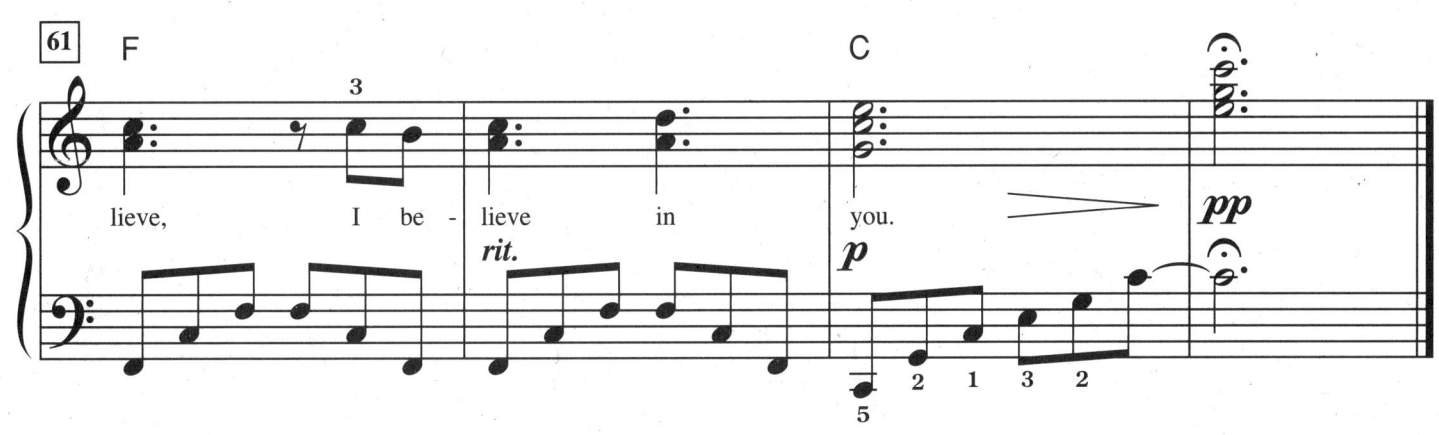

LOVE WILL ALWAYS WIN

Words and Music by
Wayne Kirkpatrick and Gordon Kennedy
Arranged by Dan Coates

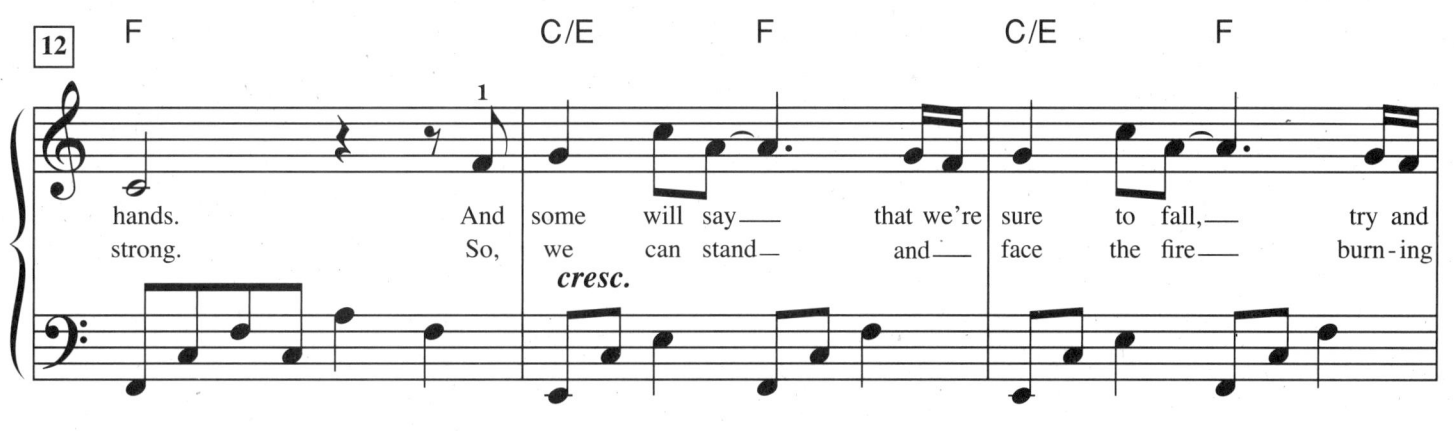
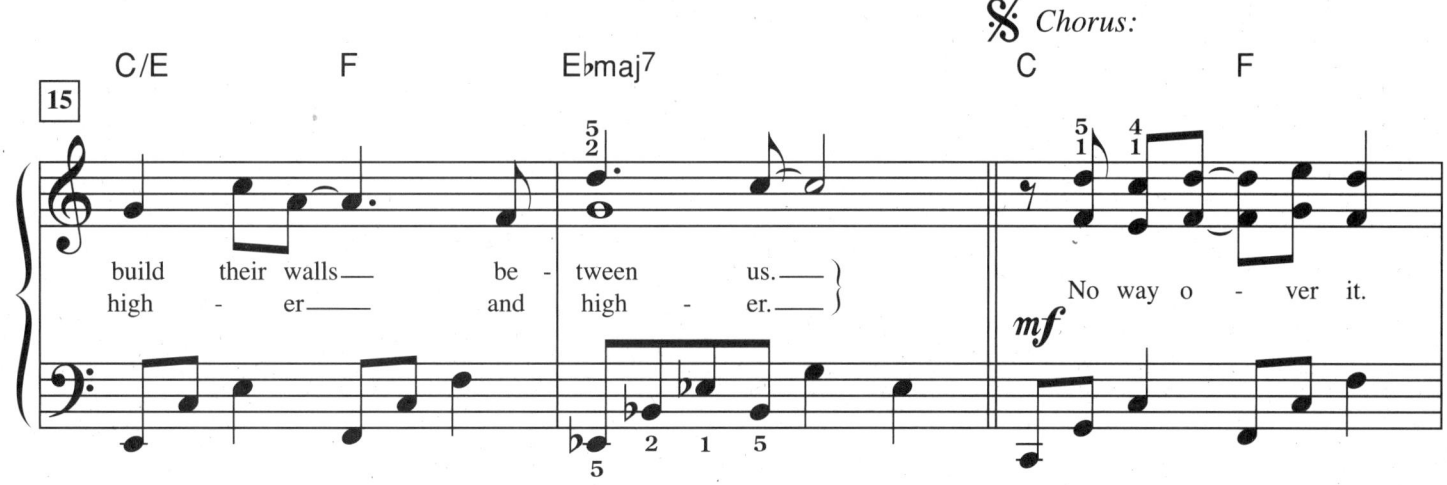

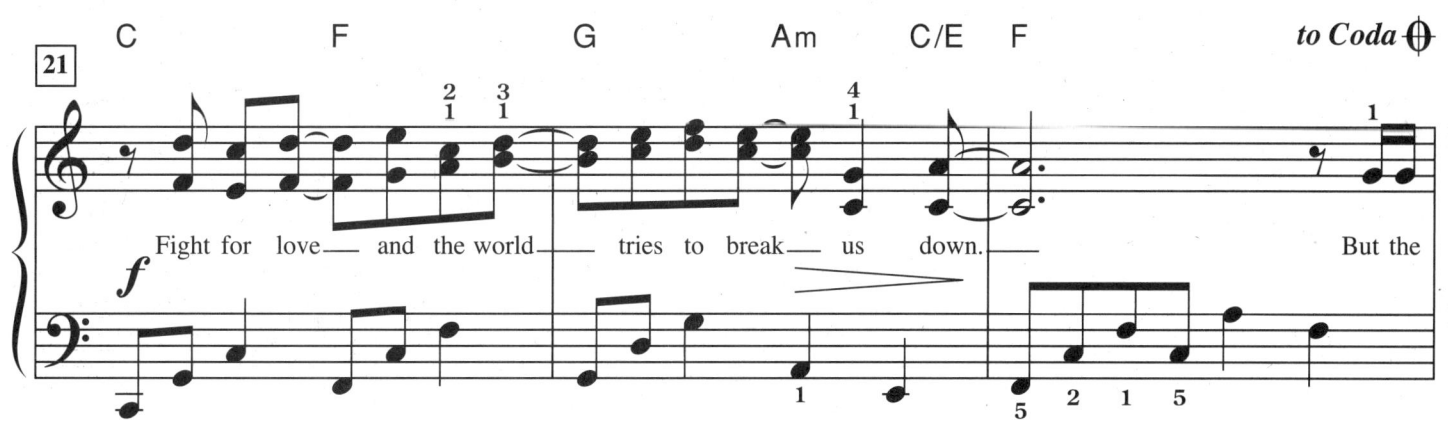

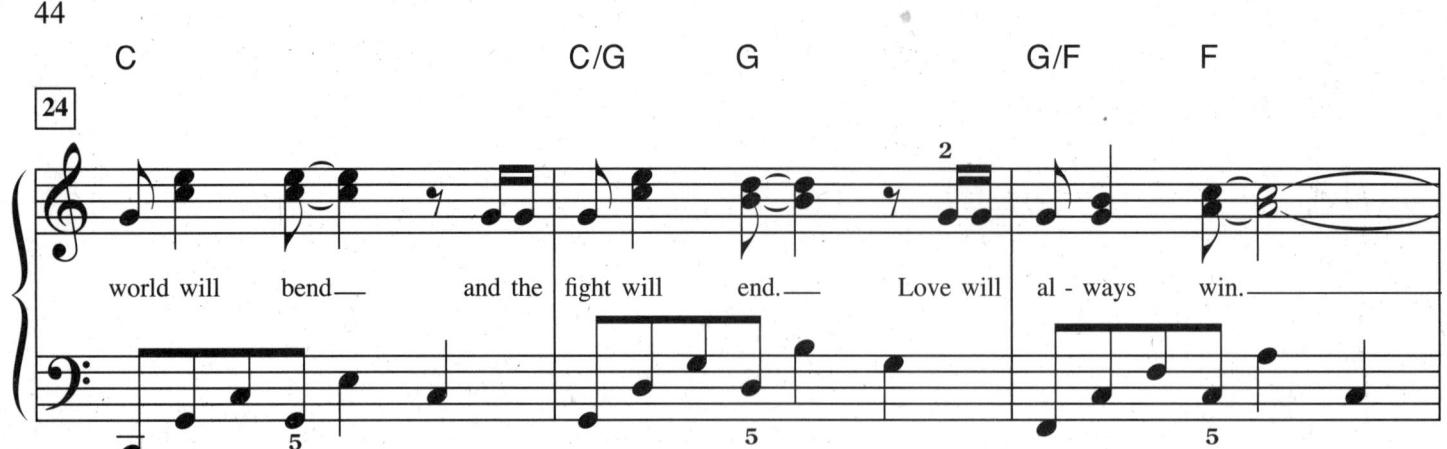
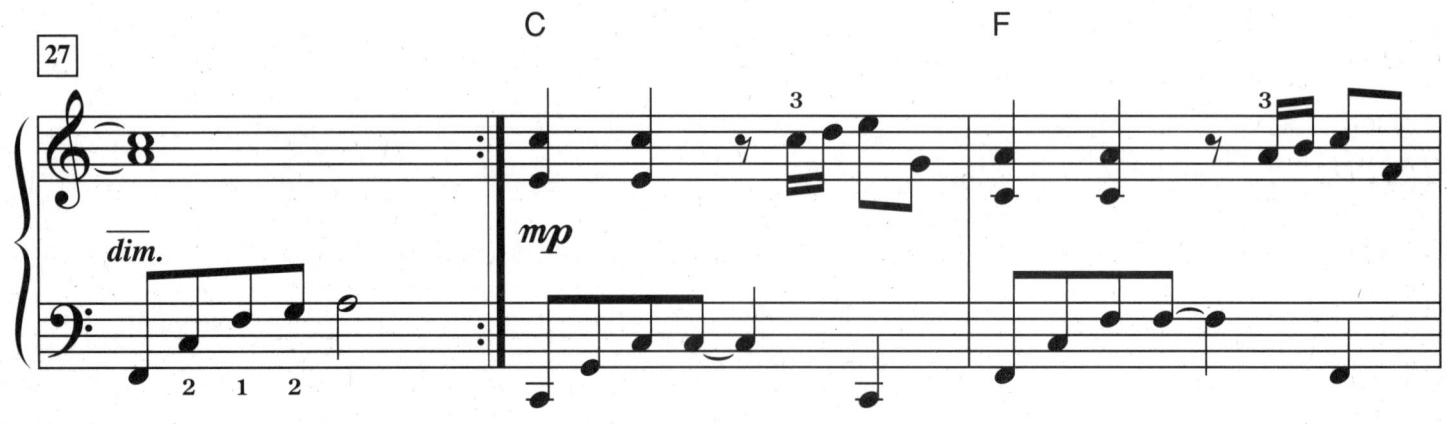
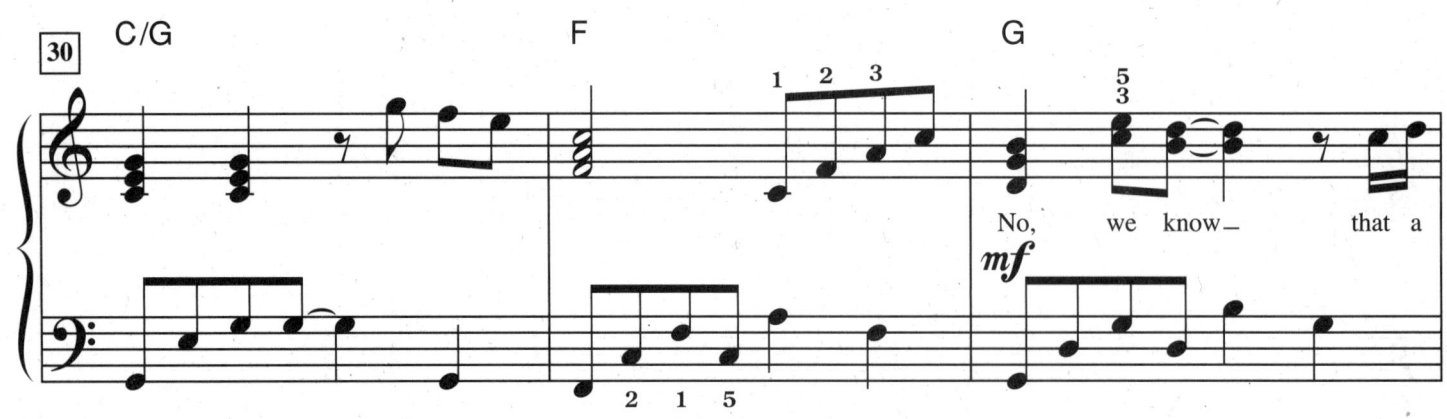
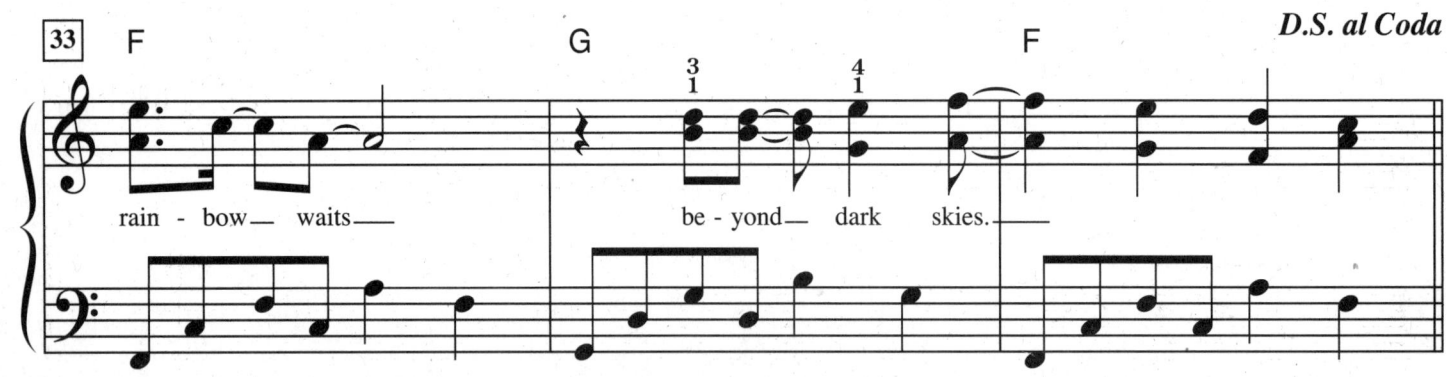

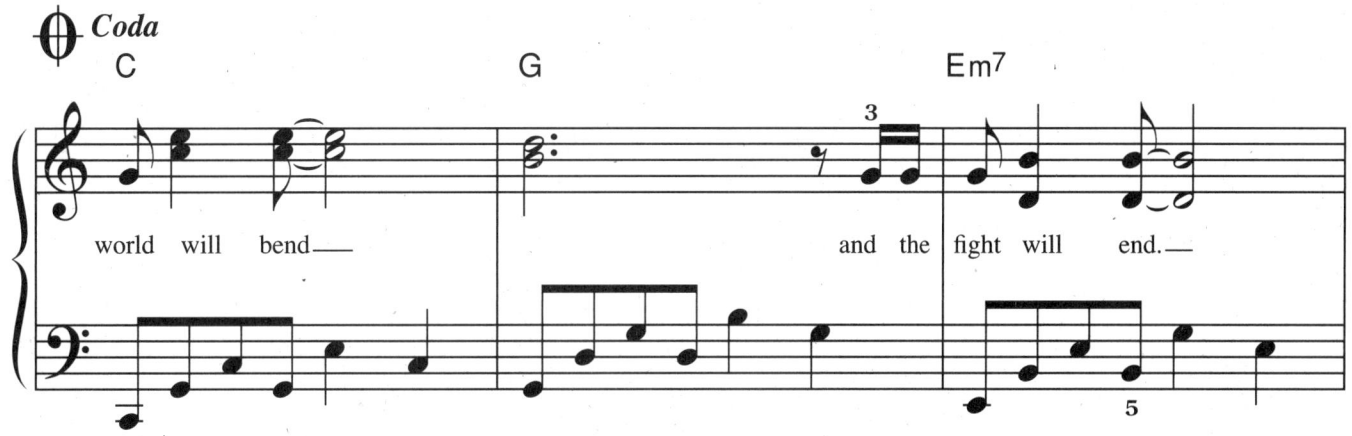

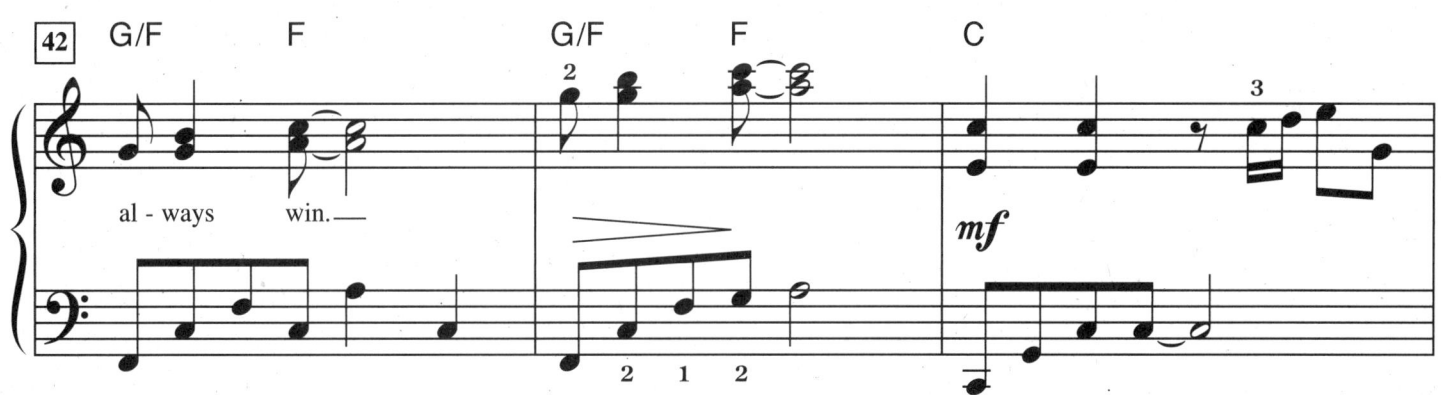
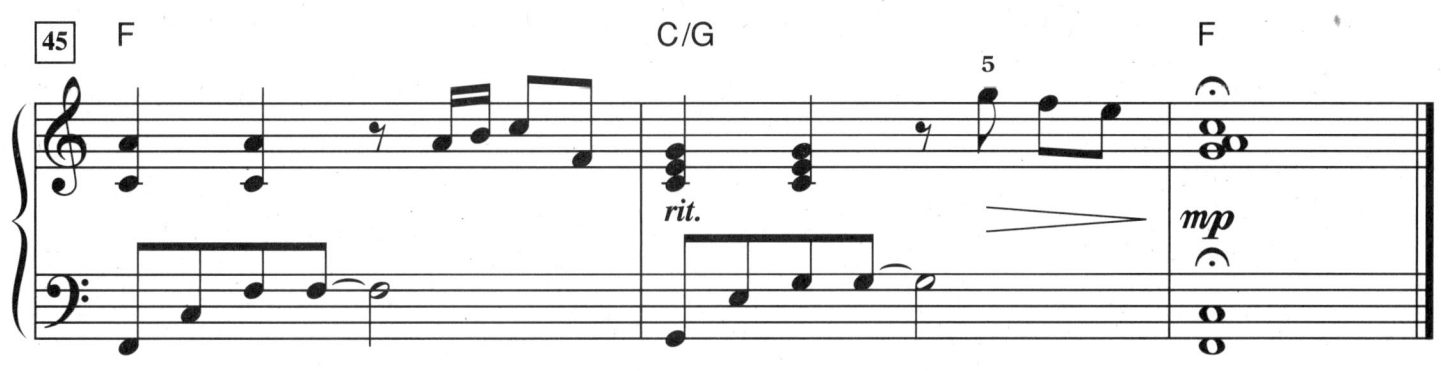

LIVE LIKE YOU WERE DYING

Words and Music by
Tim Nichols and Craig Wiseman
Arranged by Dan Coates

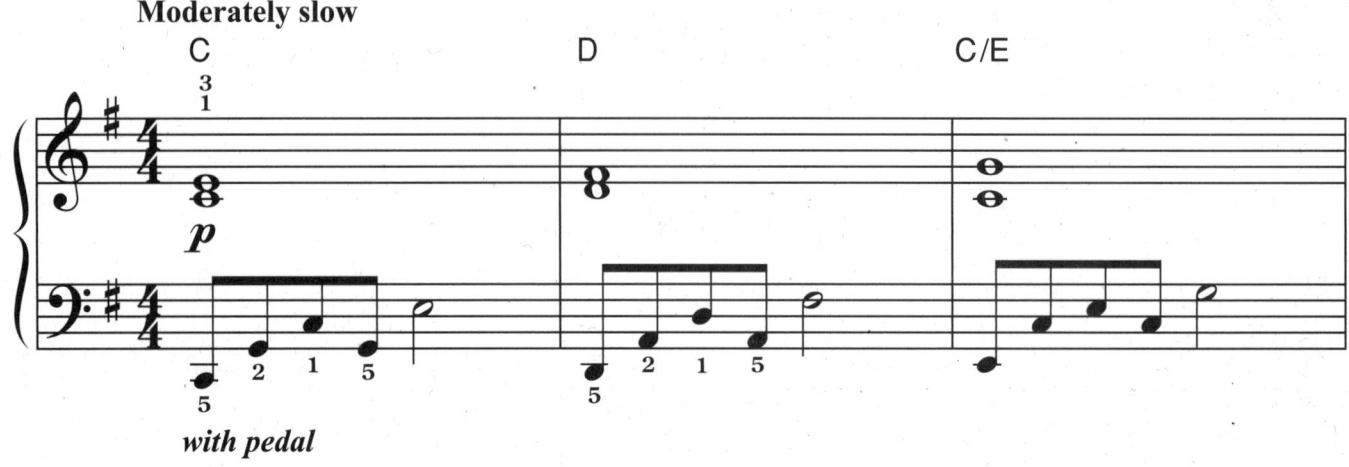

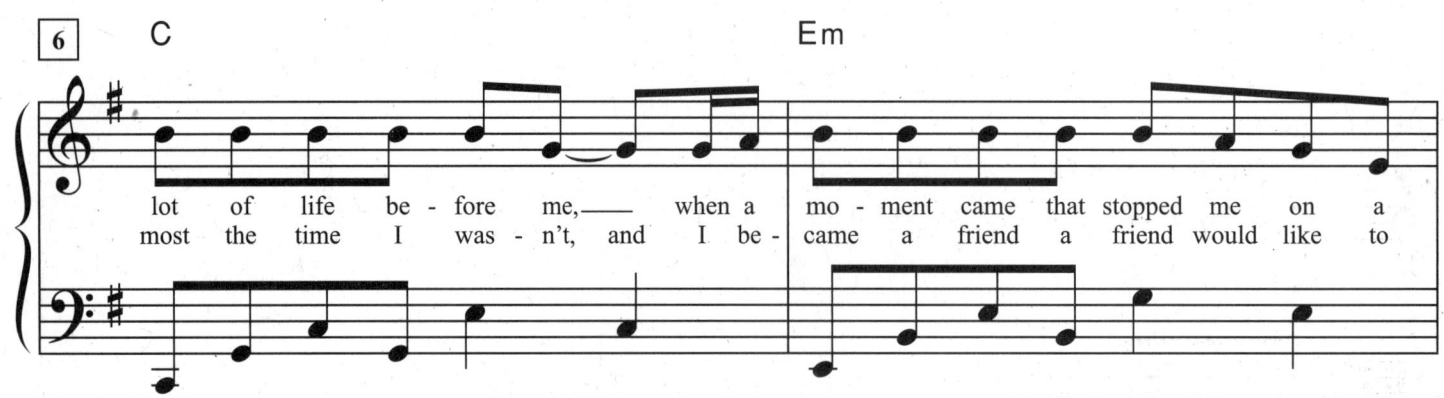

© 2004 WARNER-TAMERLANE PUBLISHING CORP. and
BIG LOUD SHIRT INDUSTRIES (Administered by BIG LOUD BUCKS, LLC) and BUG MUSIC
All Rights Reserved

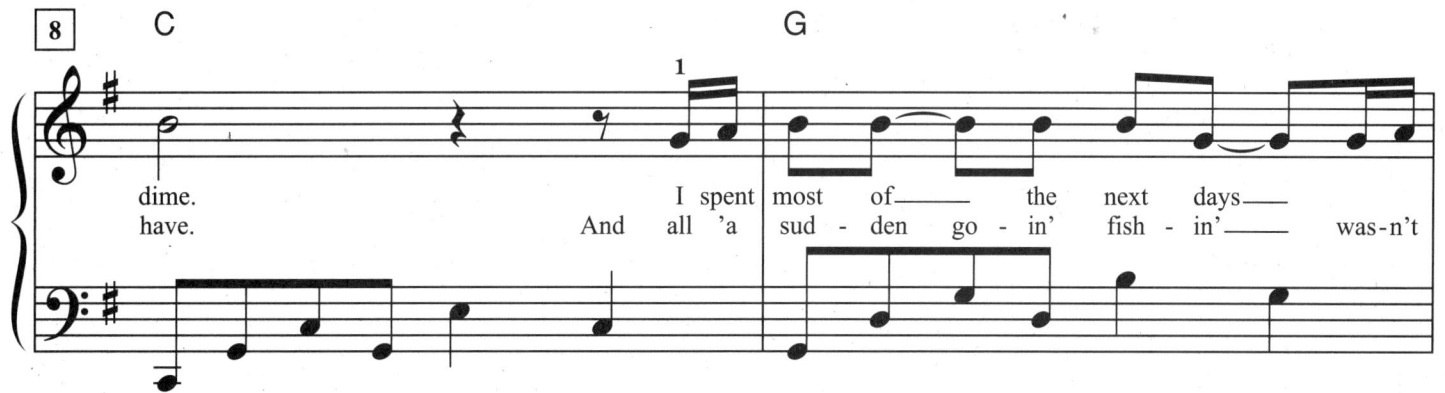
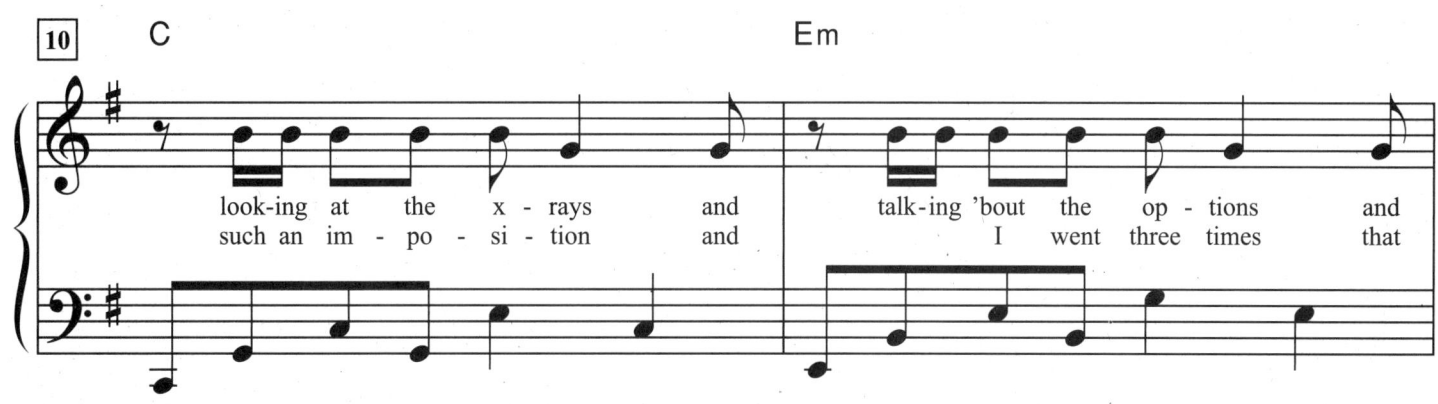

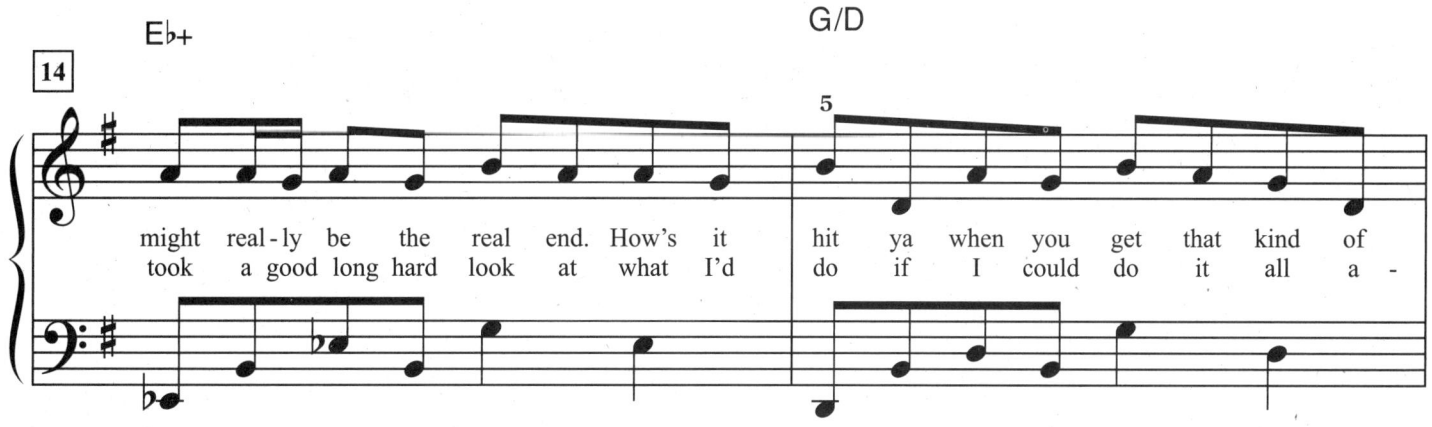

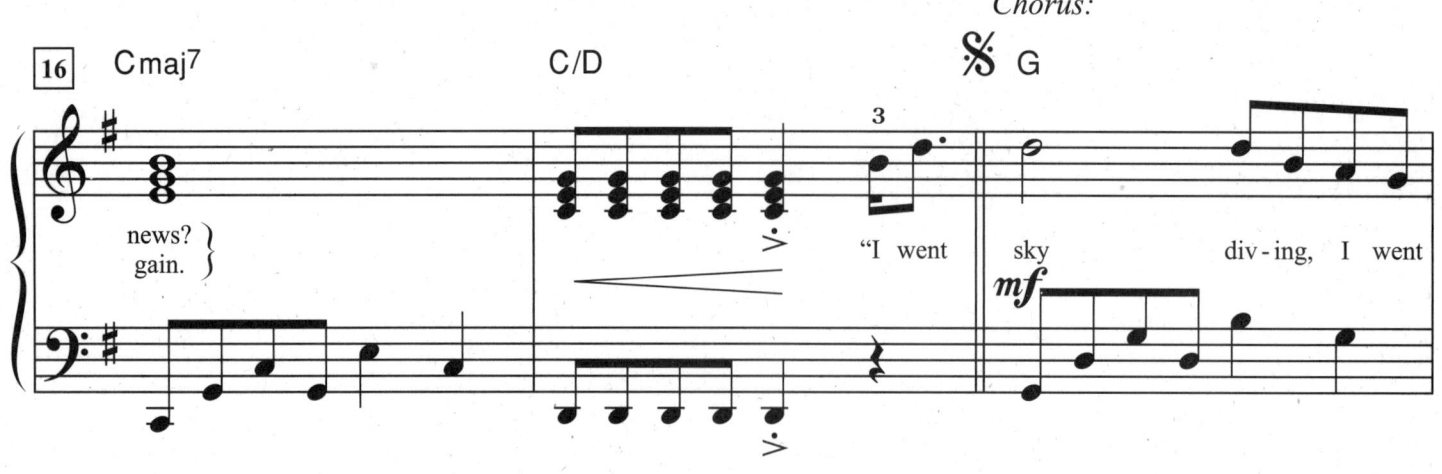
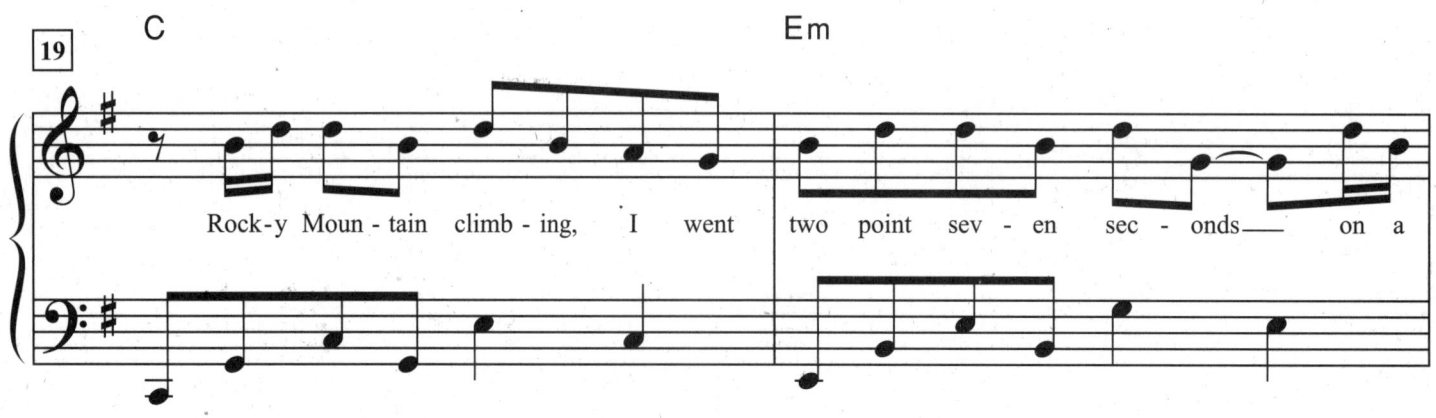

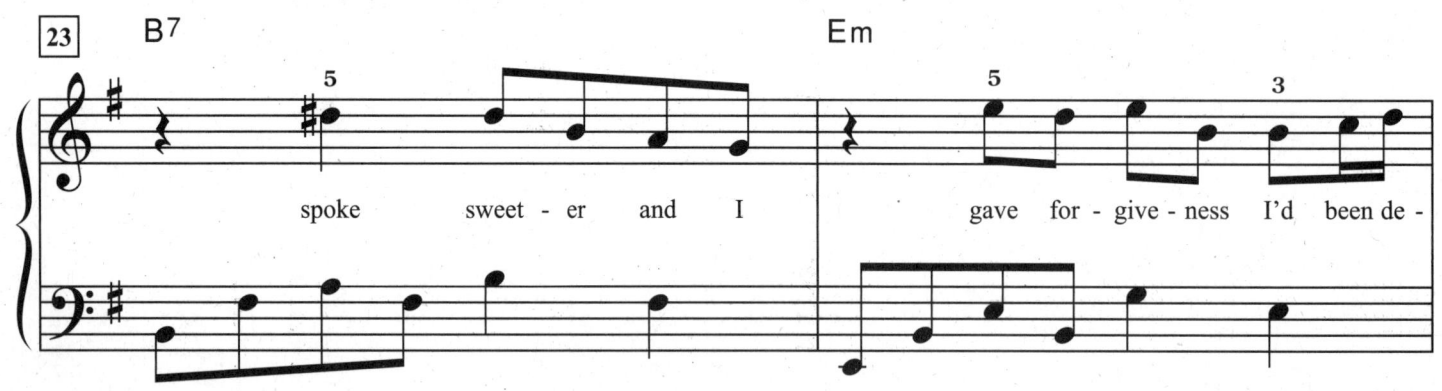

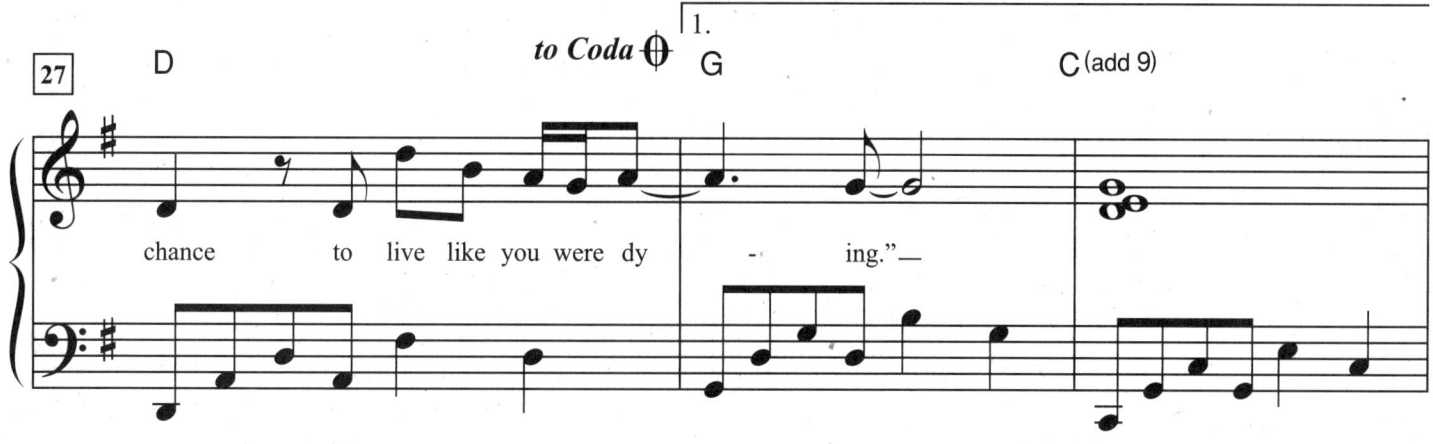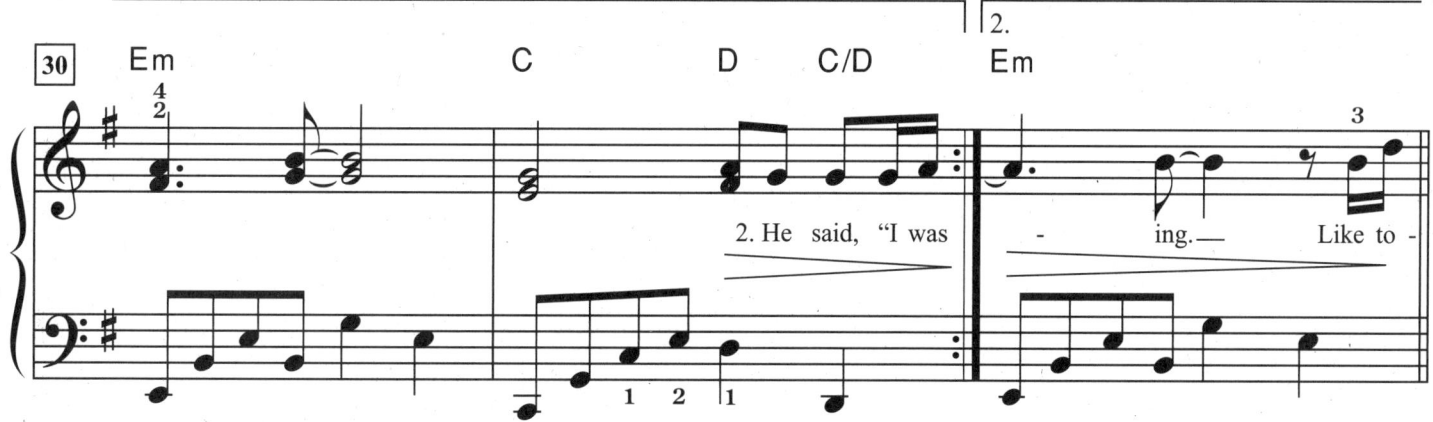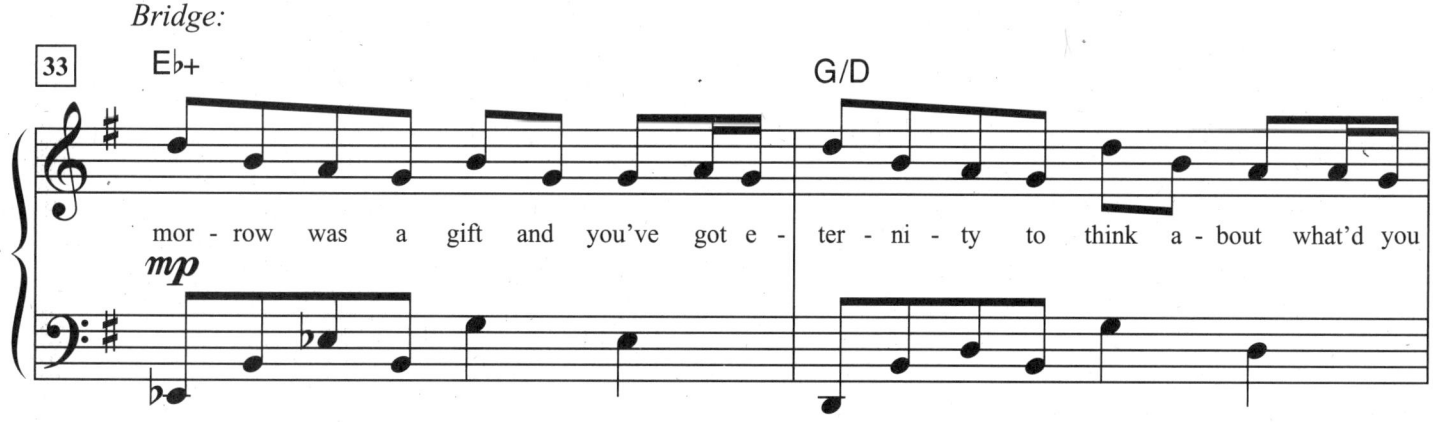

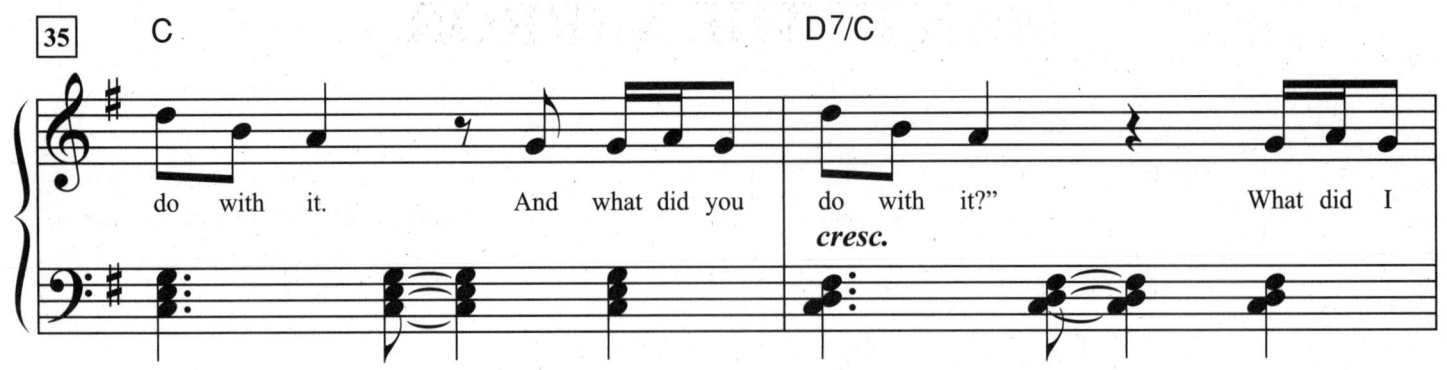

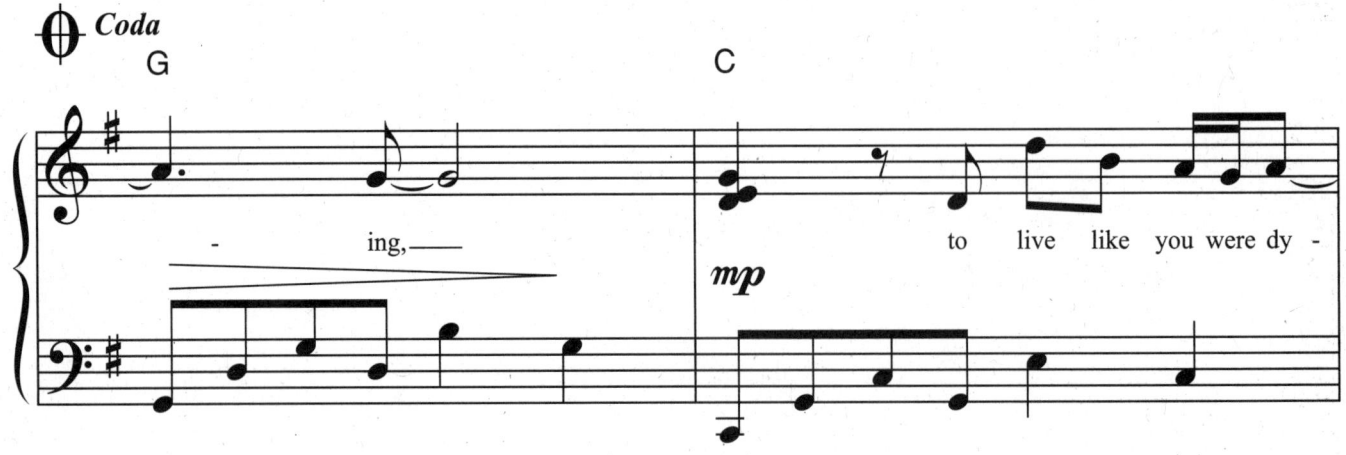

MAN IN THE MIRROR

Words and Music by
Siedah Garrett and Glen Ballard
Arranged by Dan Coates

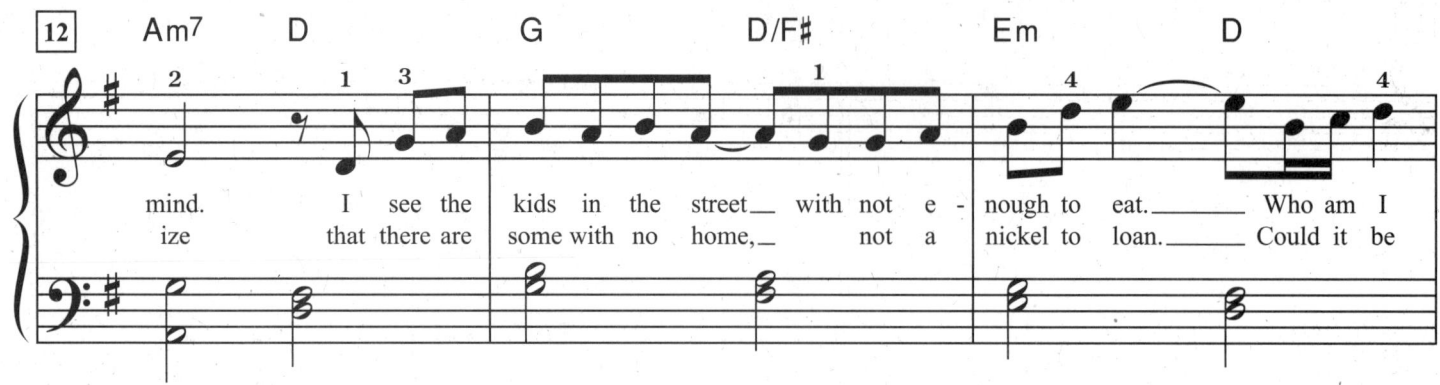

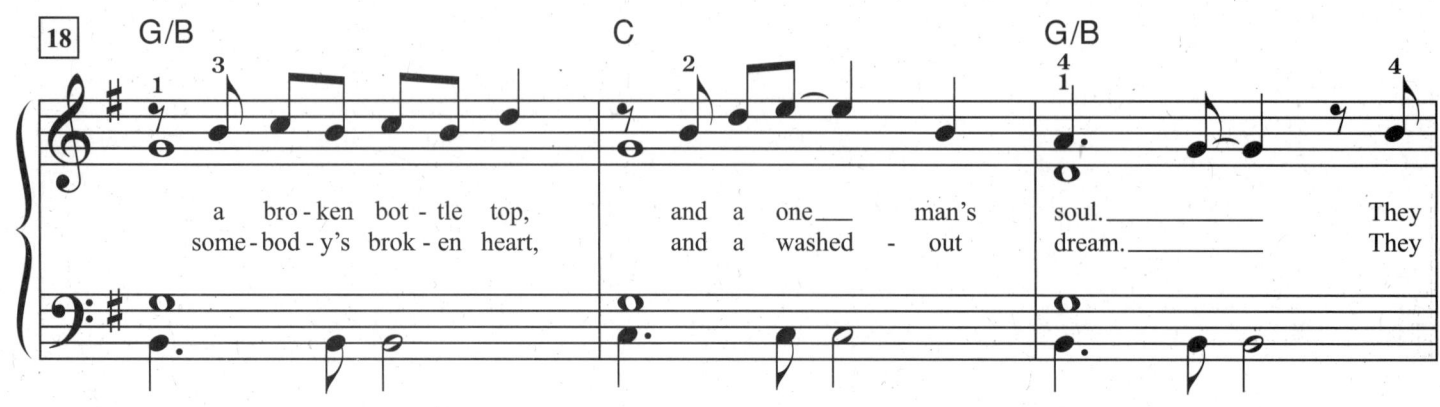

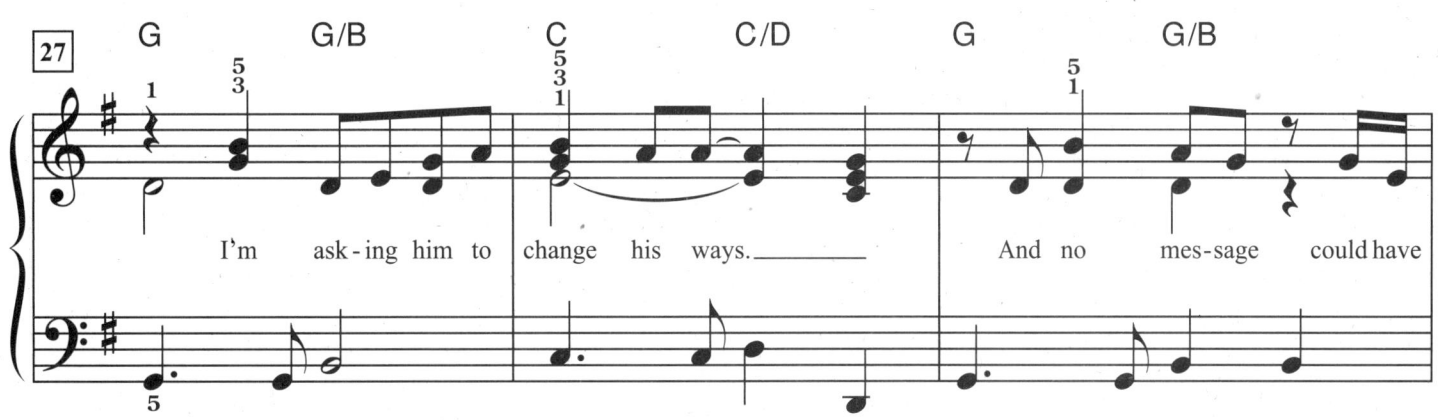

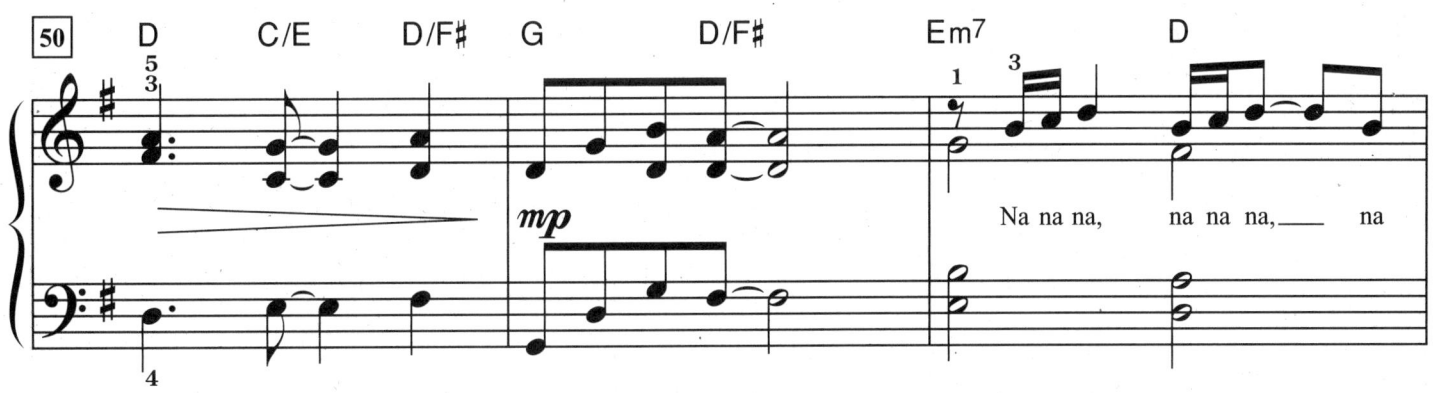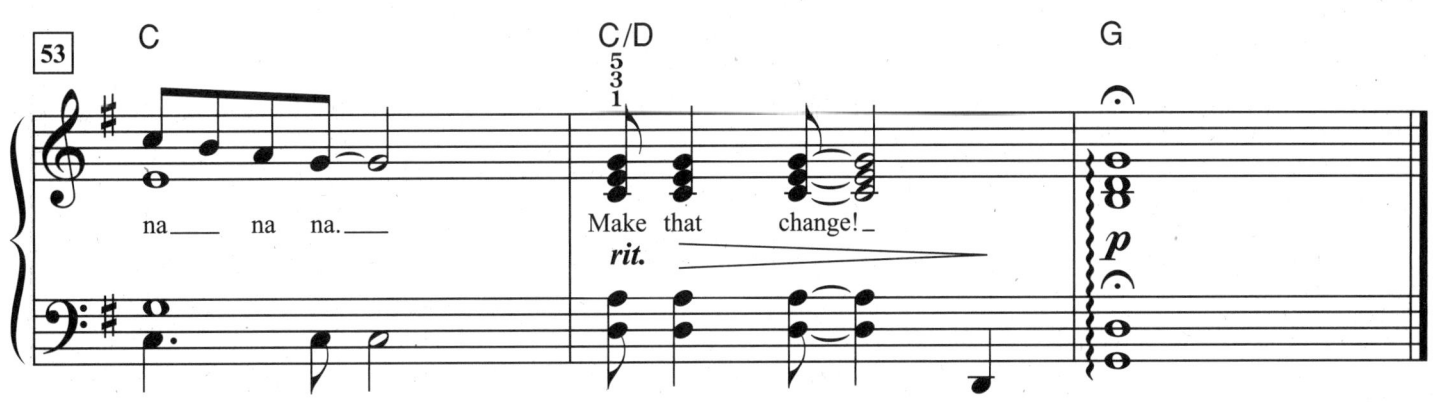

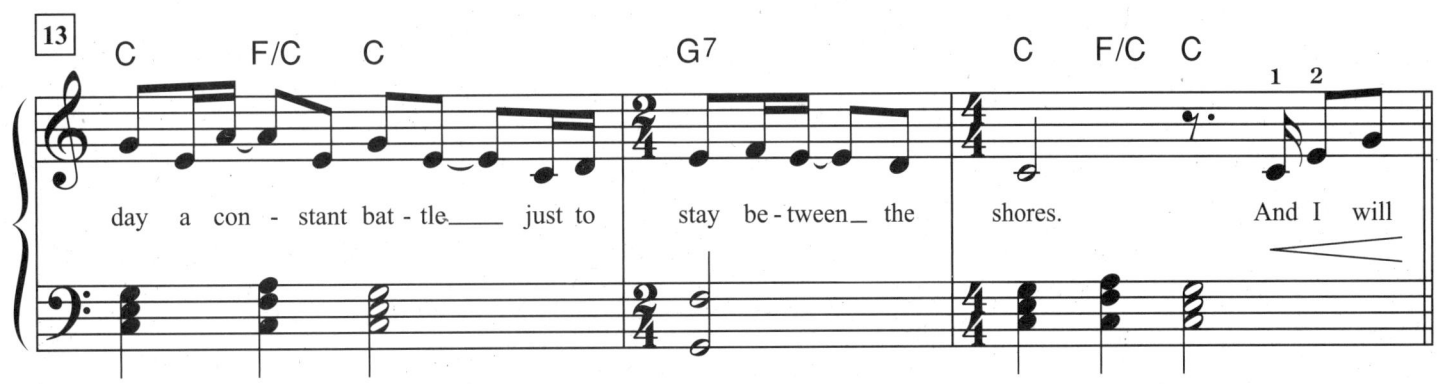
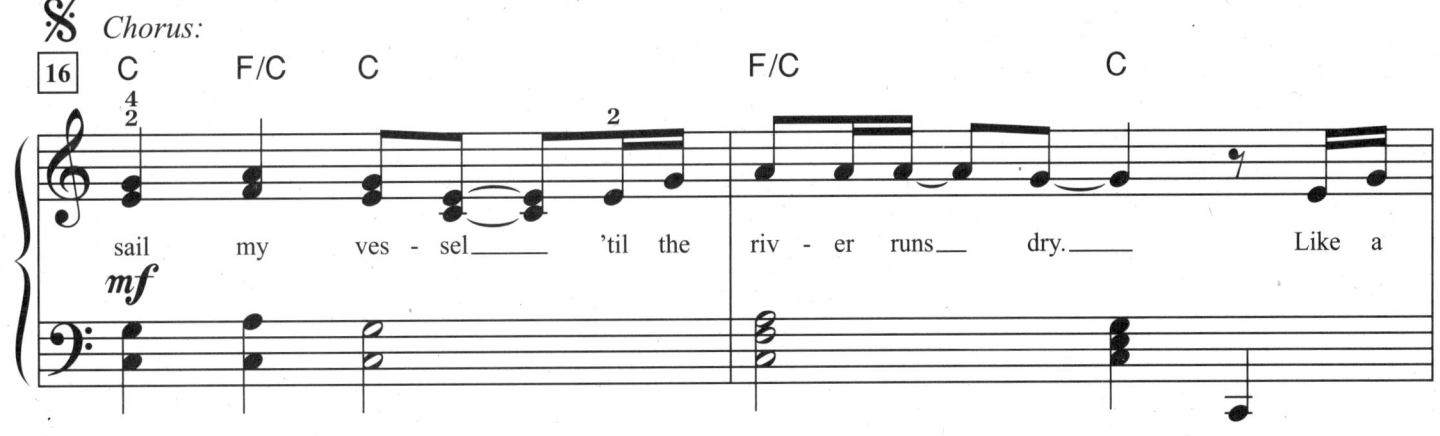
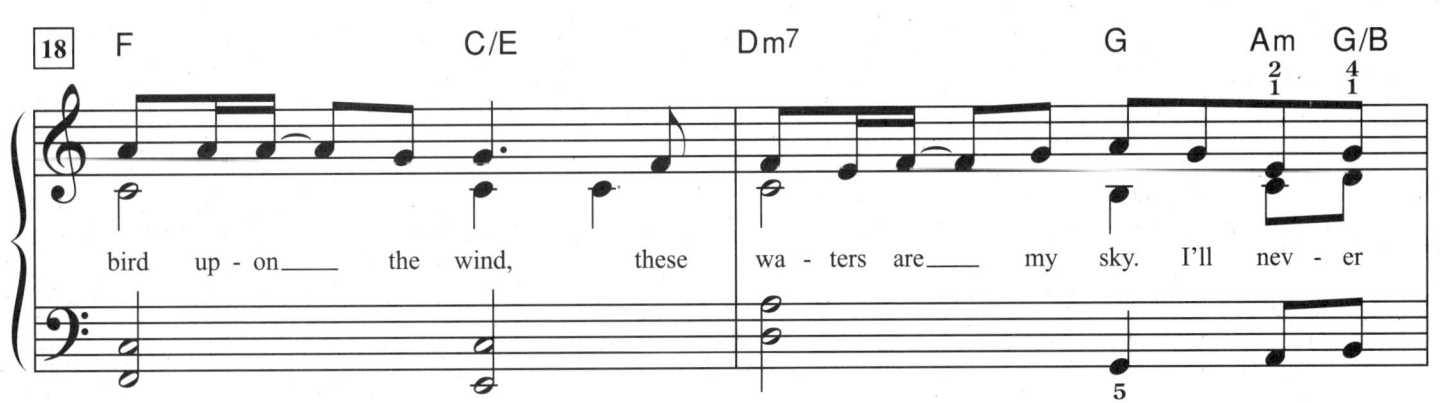

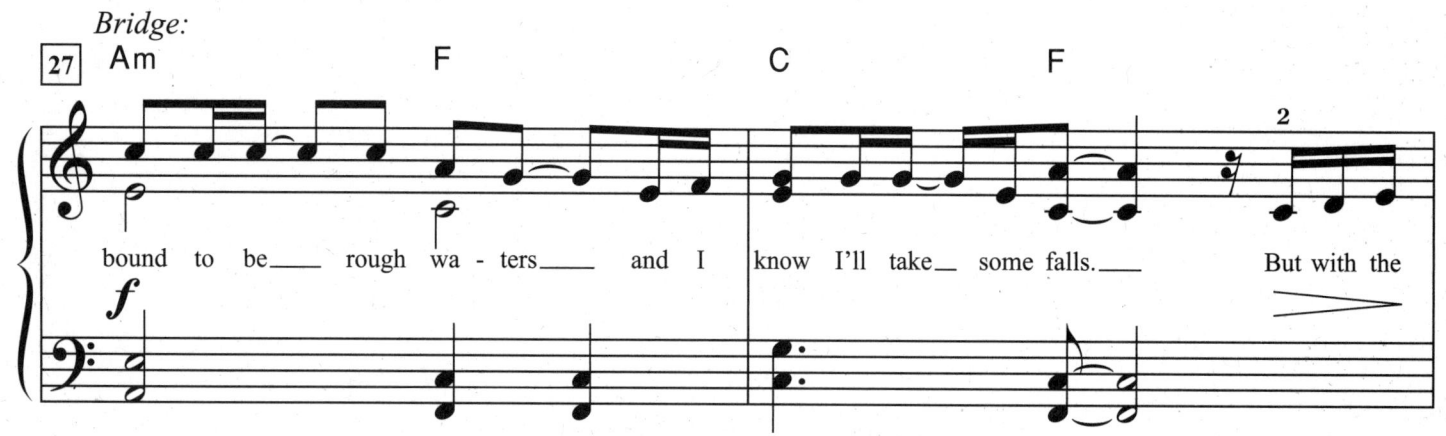

Verse 2:
Too many times we stand aside
And let the waters slip away
'Til what we put off 'til tomorrow
Has now become today.
So don't you sit upon the shoreline
And say you're satisfied.
Choose to chance the rapids
And dare to dance the tide.
Yes I will…
(To Chorus:)

TO WHERE YOU ARE

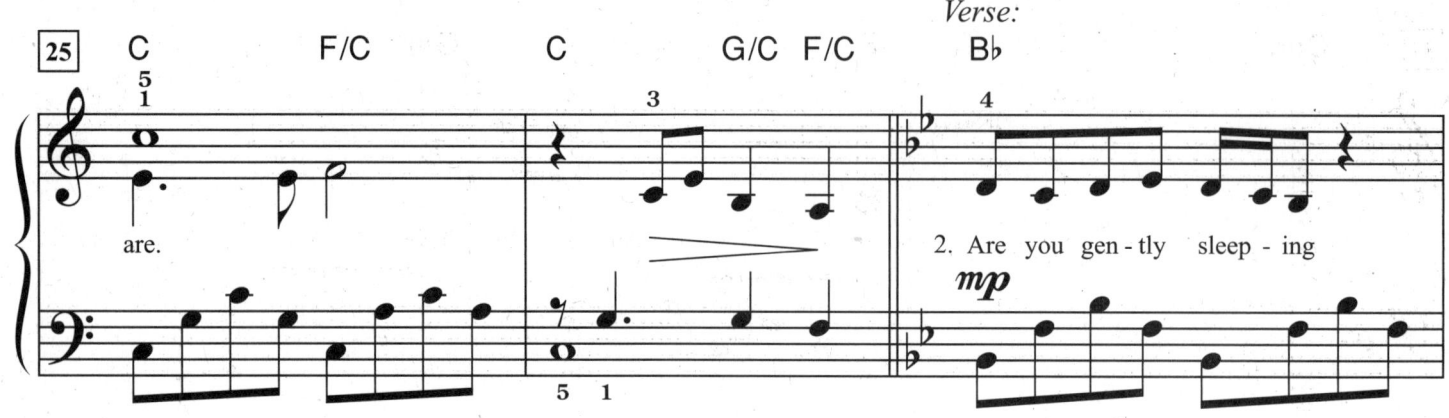

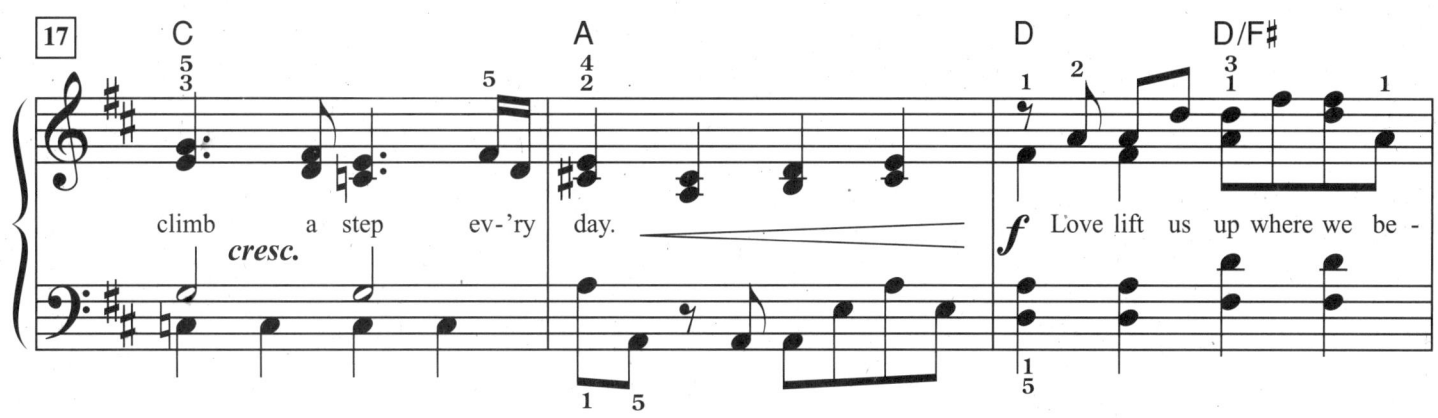
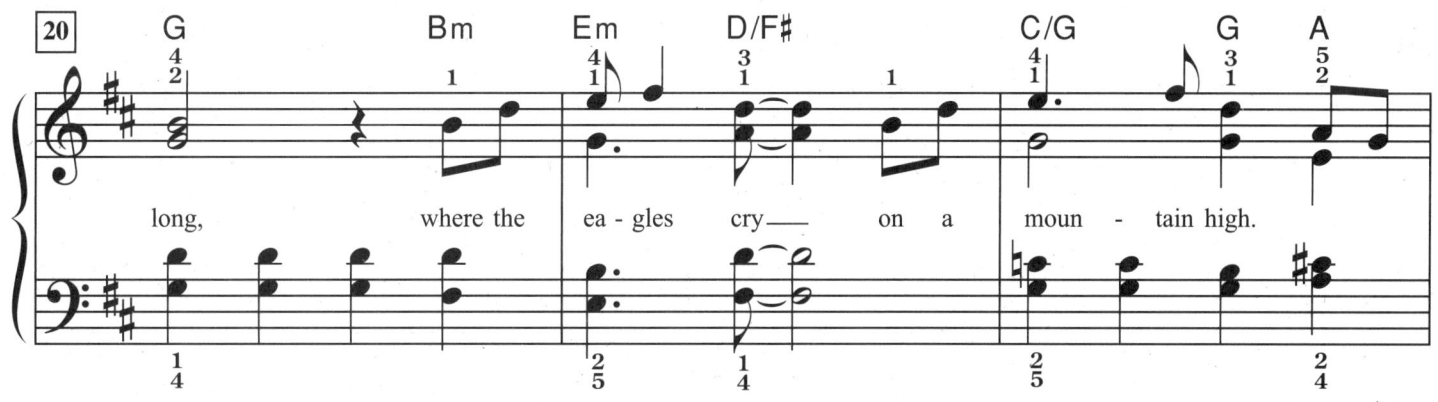
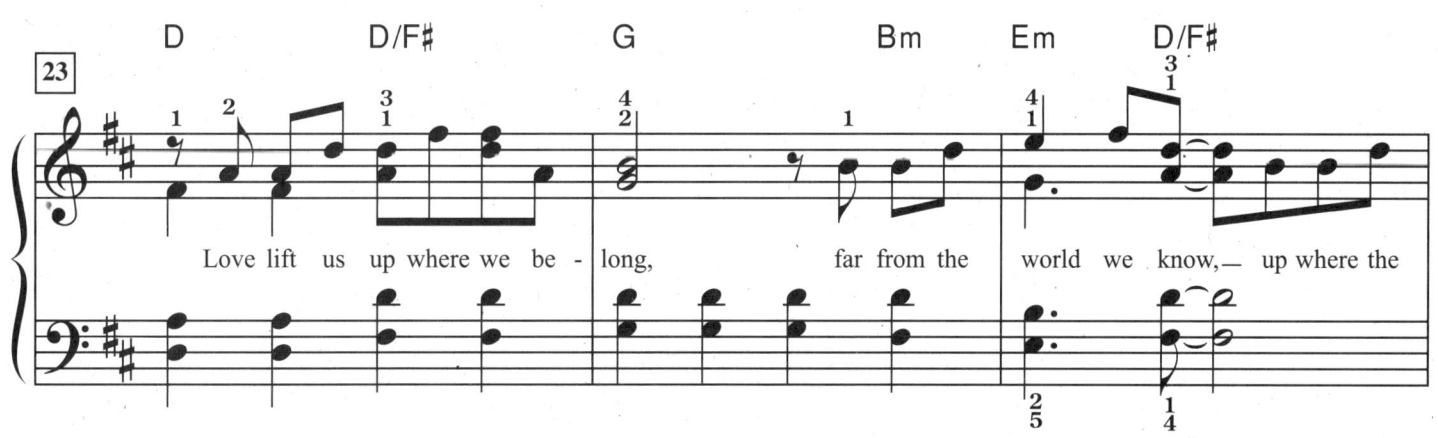

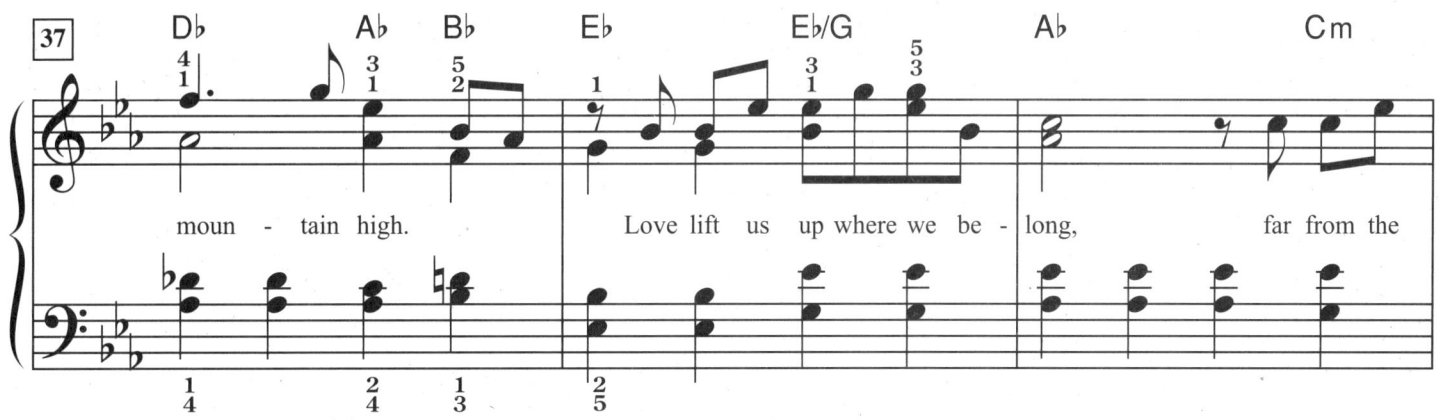
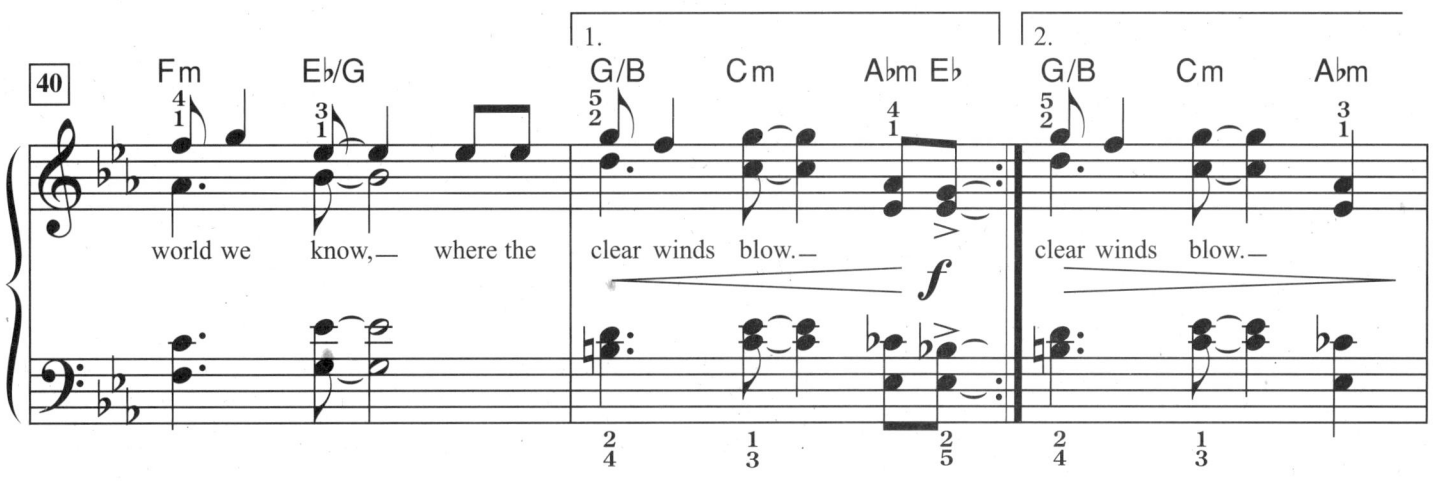

Verse 2:
Some hang on to "used-to-be,"
Live their lives looking behind.
All we have is here and now;
All our life, out there to find.
The road is long.
There are mountains in our way,
But we climb them a step every day.

WILL YOU BE THERE
(RADIO EDIT)

Written and Composed by Michael Jackson
Arranged by Dan Coates

© 1991 MIJAC MUSIC (BMI)
All Rights Administered by WARNER-TAMERLANE PUBLISHING CORP. (BMI)
All Rights Reserved   From the Original Motion Picture Soundtrack "FREE WILLIE"

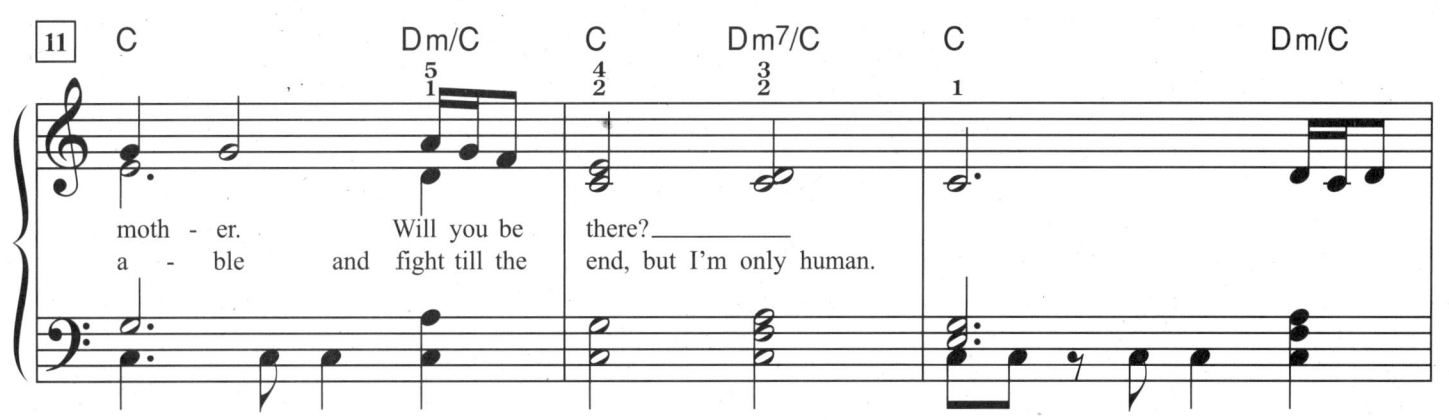
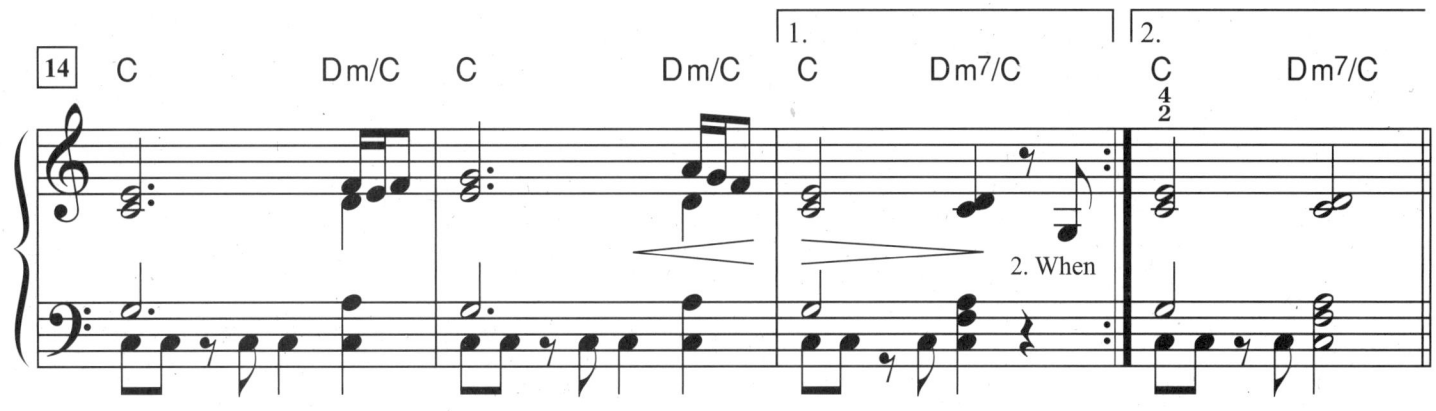
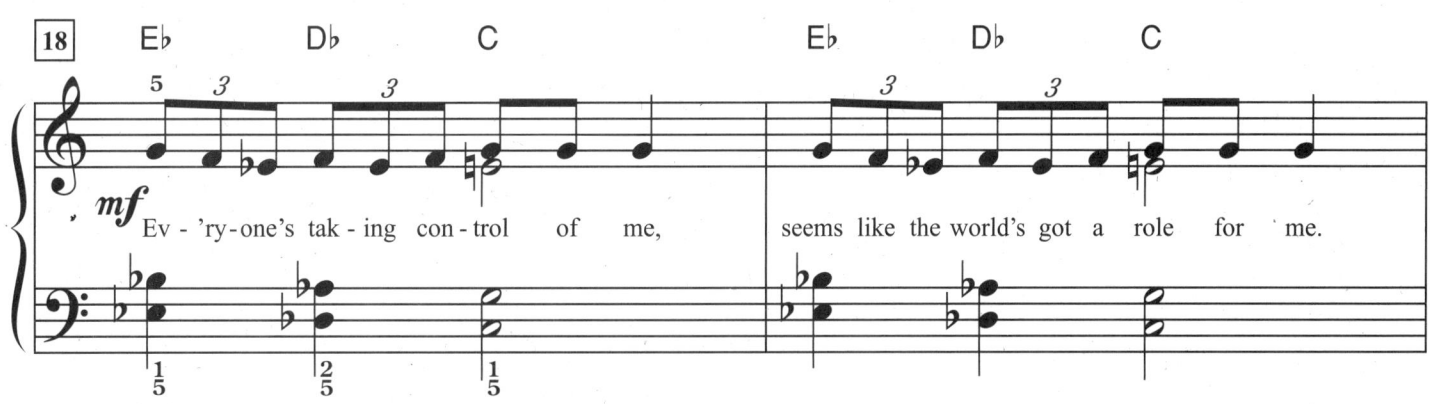

THE WIND BENEATH MY WINGS

(from "Beaches")

Words and Music by
Larry Henley and Jeff Silbar
Arranged by Dan Coates

© 1982 WARNER HOUSE OF MUSIC and WB GOLD MUSIC CORP.
All Rights Reserved

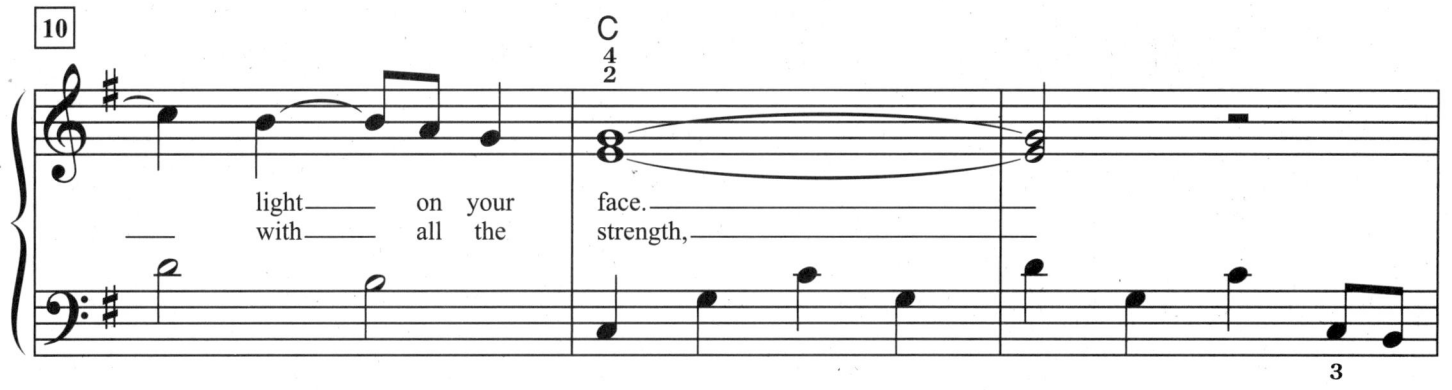
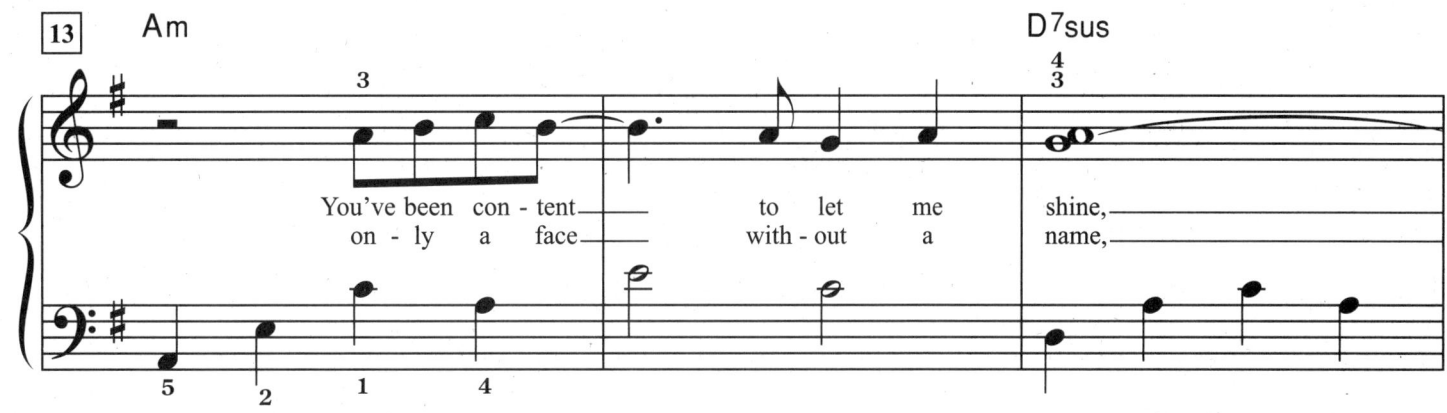

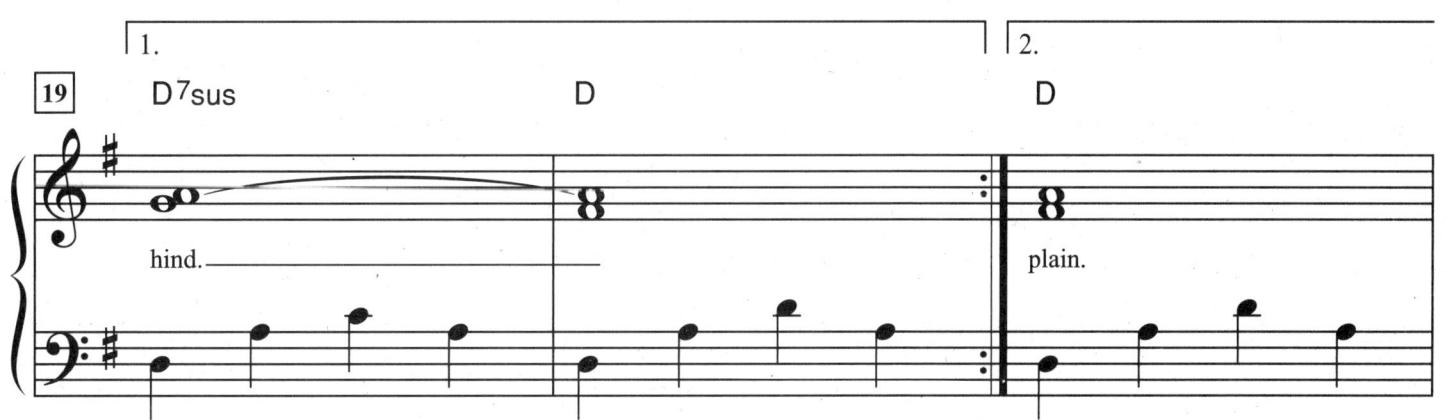

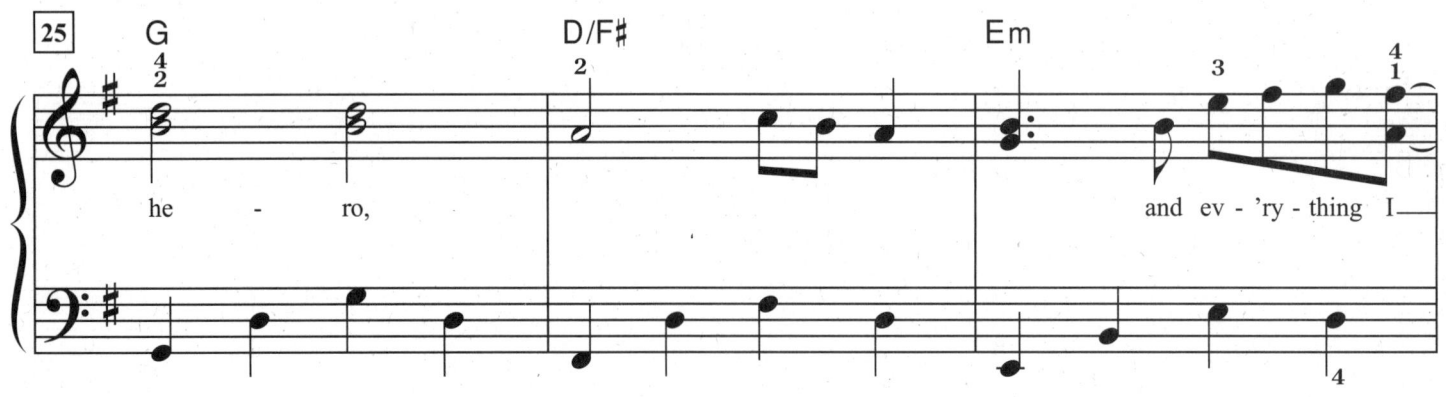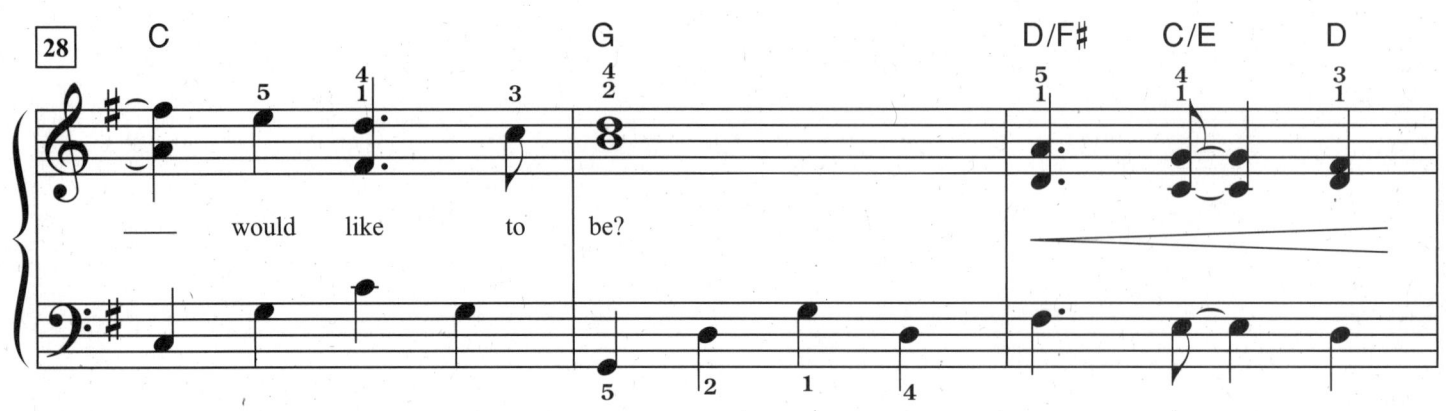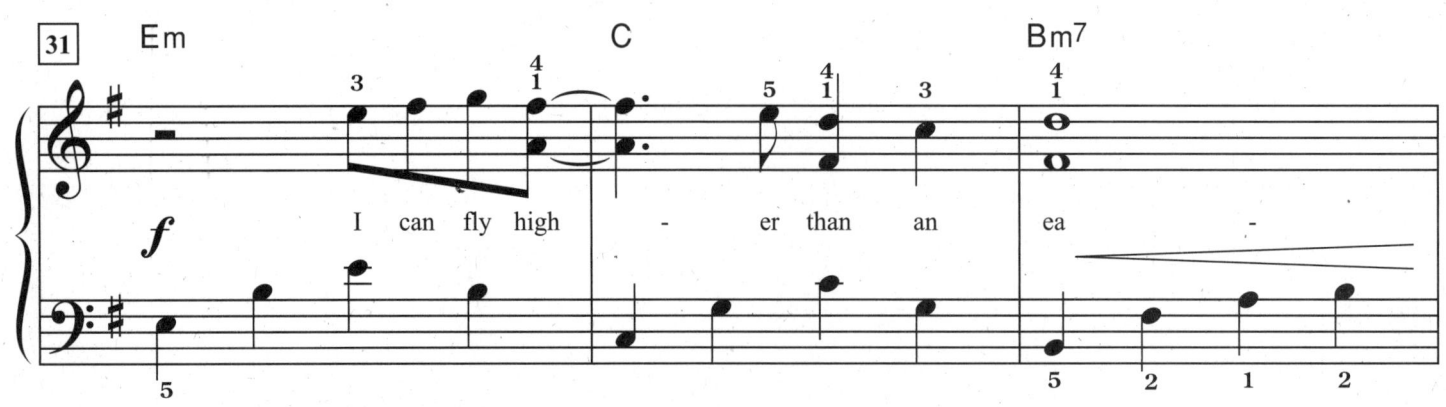

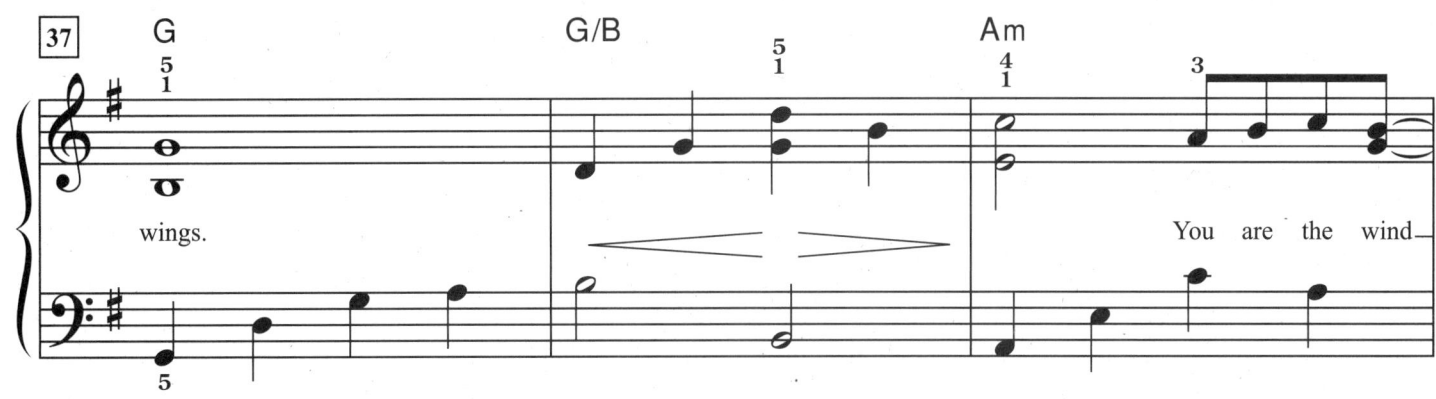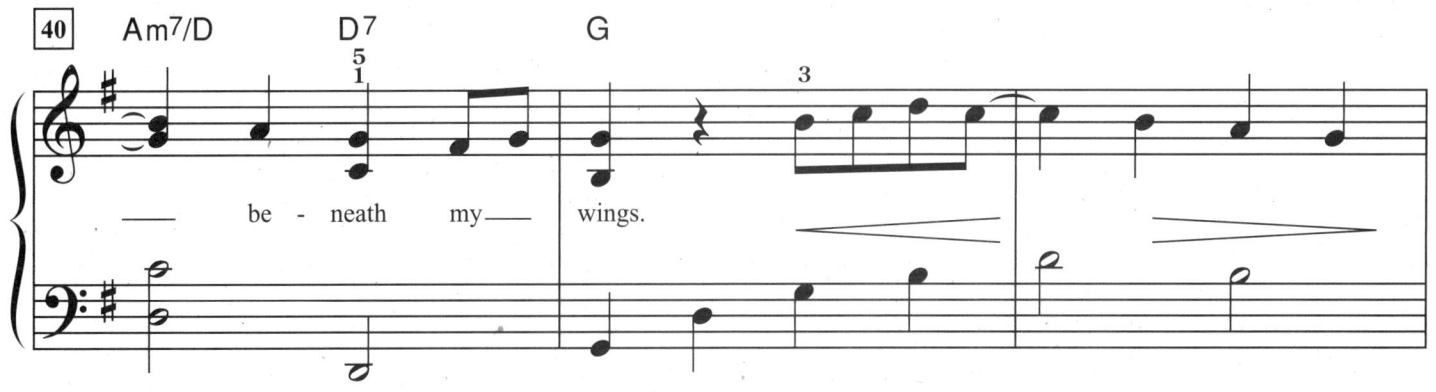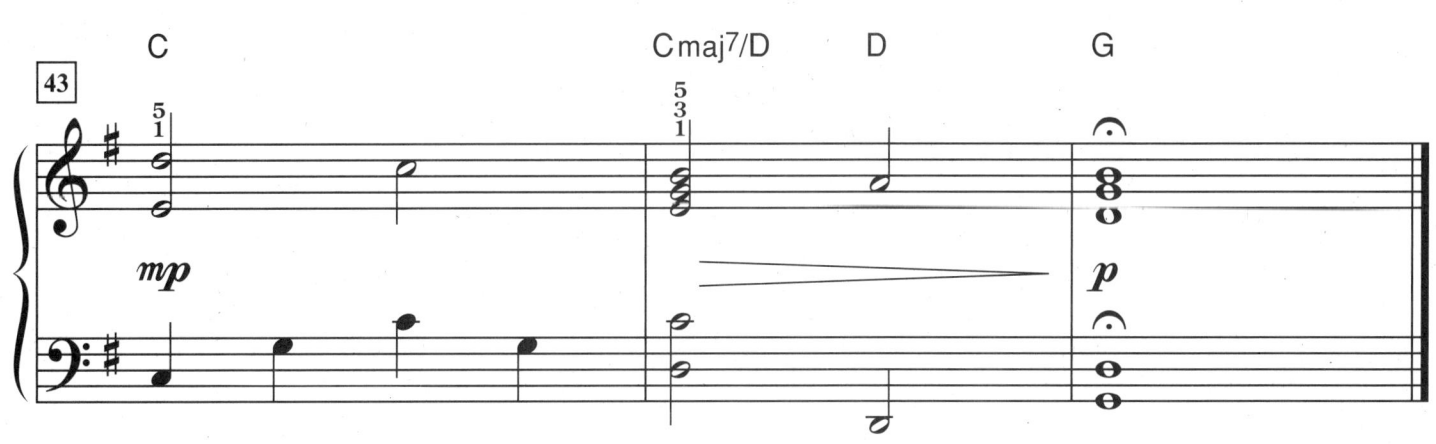

YOU HAVEN'T SEEN THE LAST OF ME

(from "Burlesque")

Words and Music by Diane Warren
Arranged by Dan Coates

© 2010 REALSONGS (ASCAP)
All Rights Reserved

81

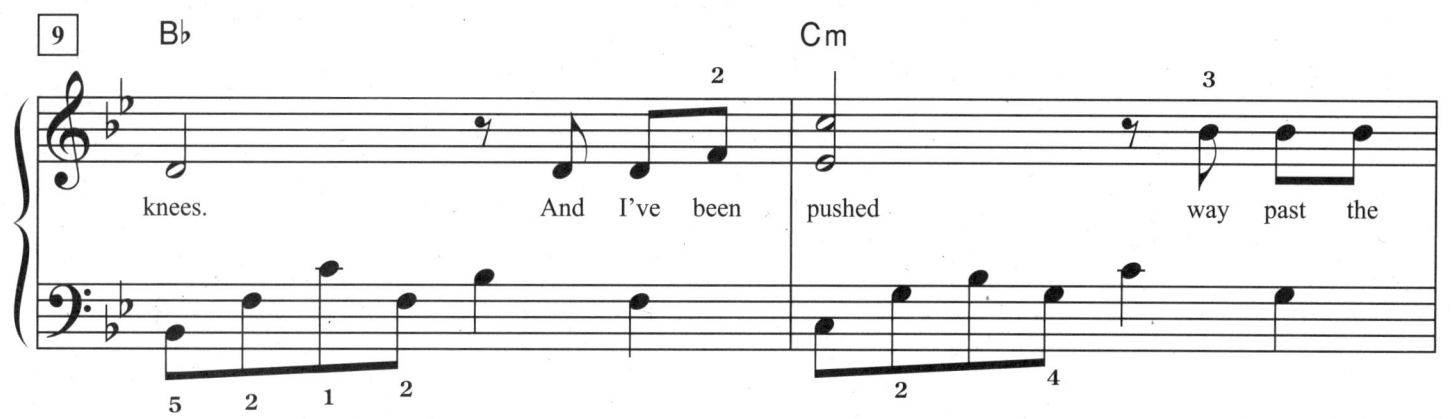

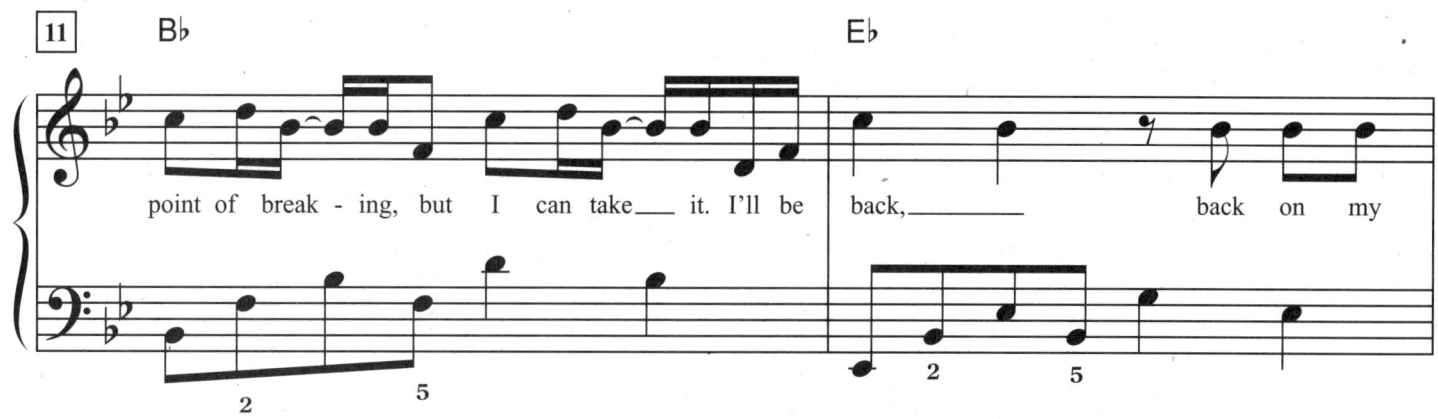

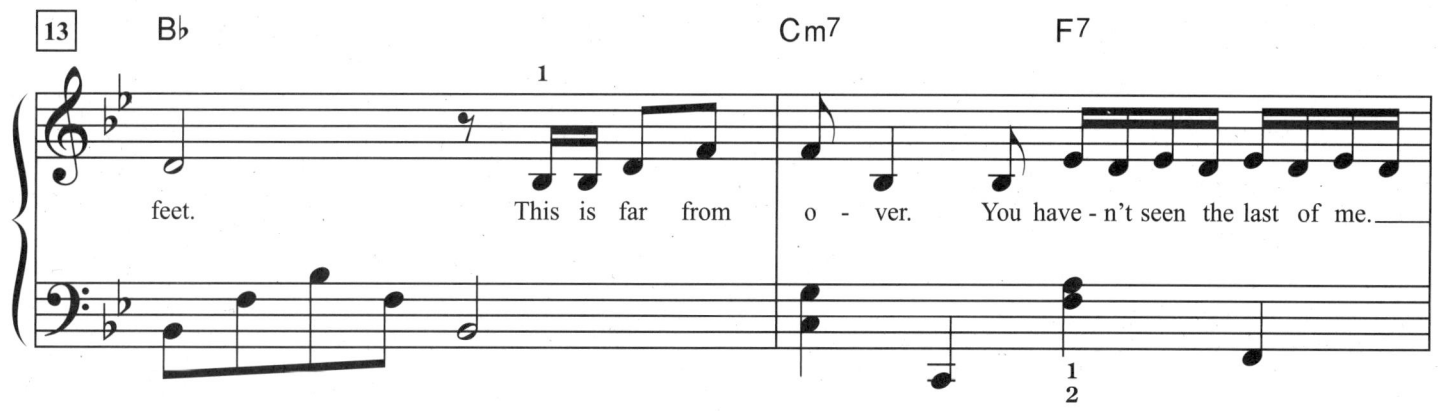

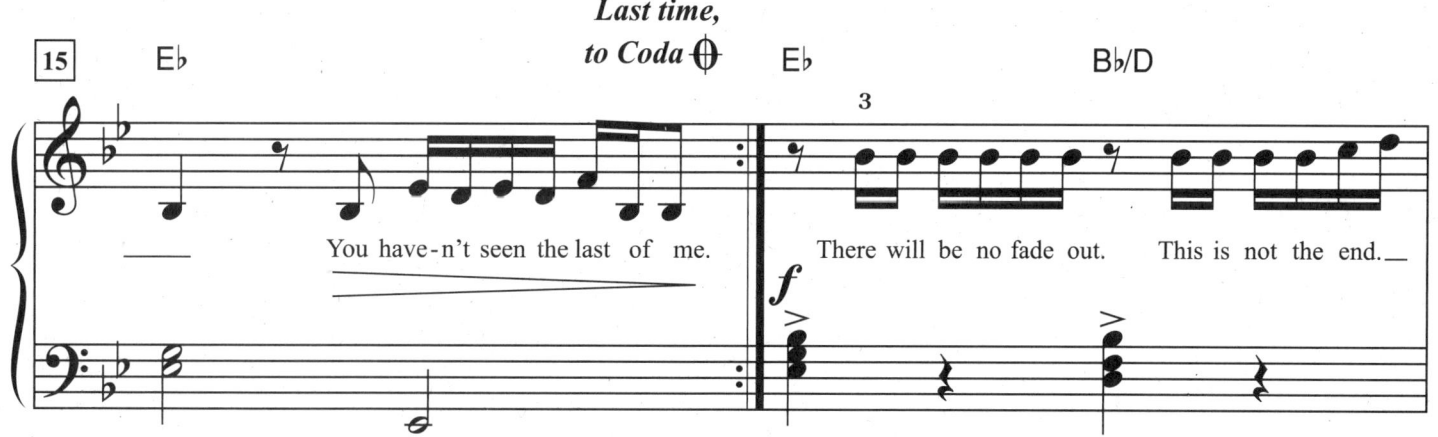

82

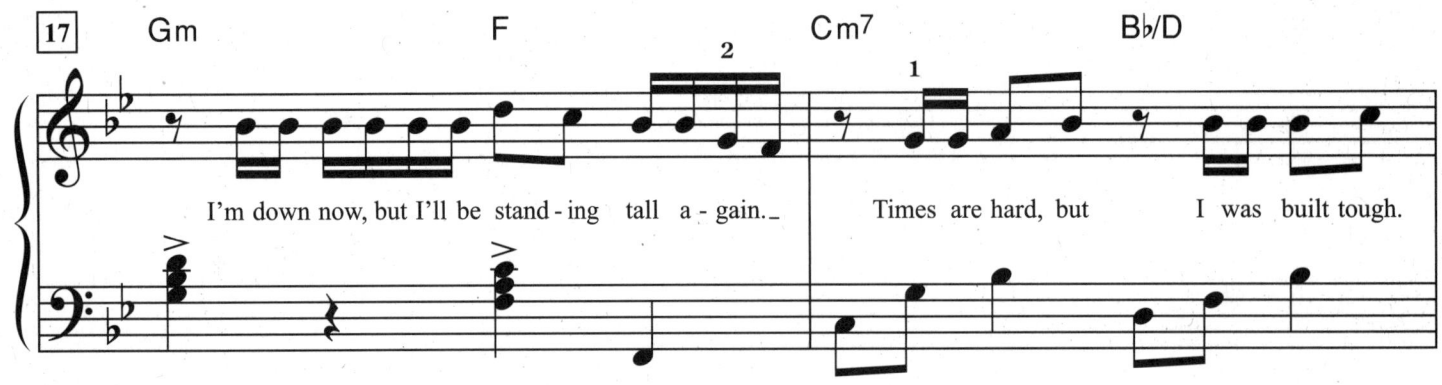

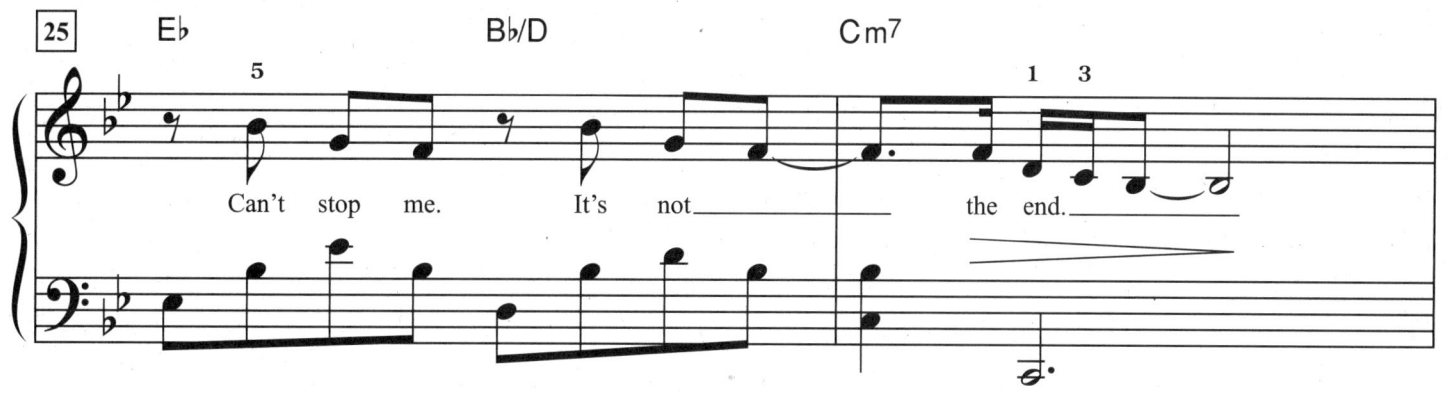
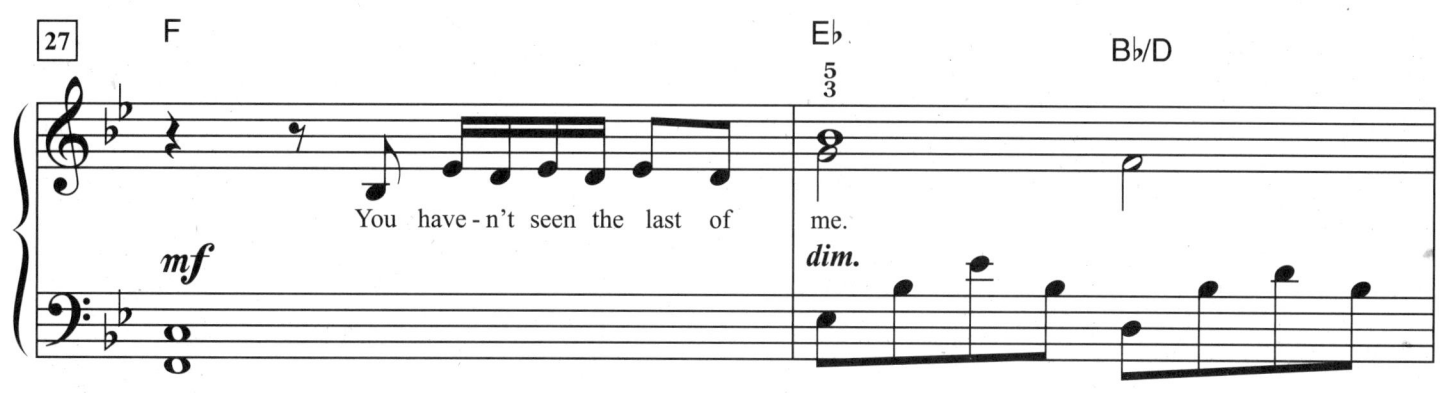

Verse 2:
They can say that I won't stay around,
But I'm gonna stand my ground.
You're not gonna stop me.
You don't know me, you don't know who I am.
Don't count me out so fast.
(To Chorus:)

YOU LIGHT UP MY LIFE

Words and Music by Joe Brooks
Arranged by Dan Coates

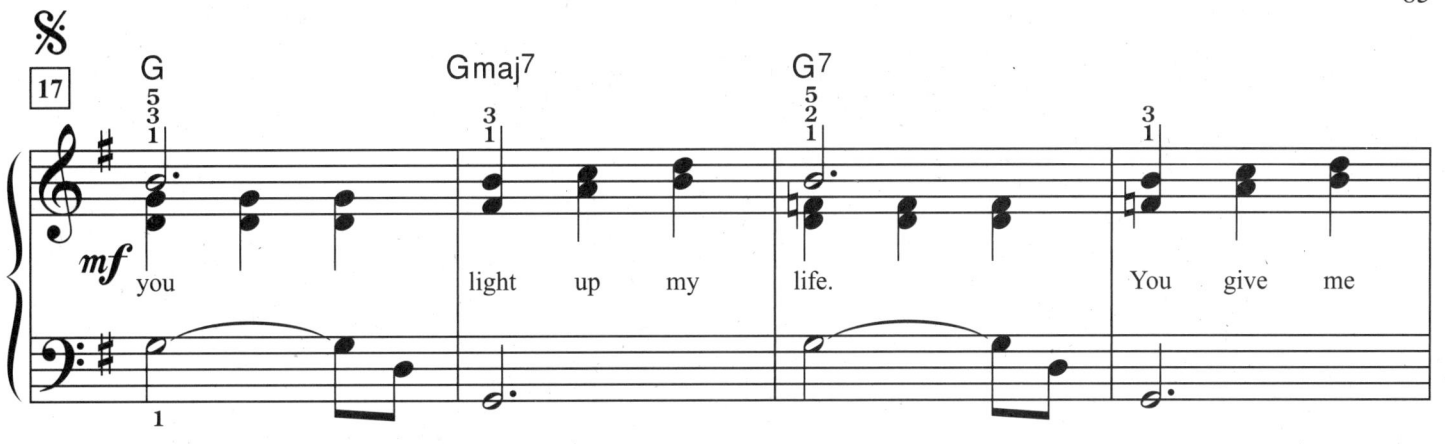
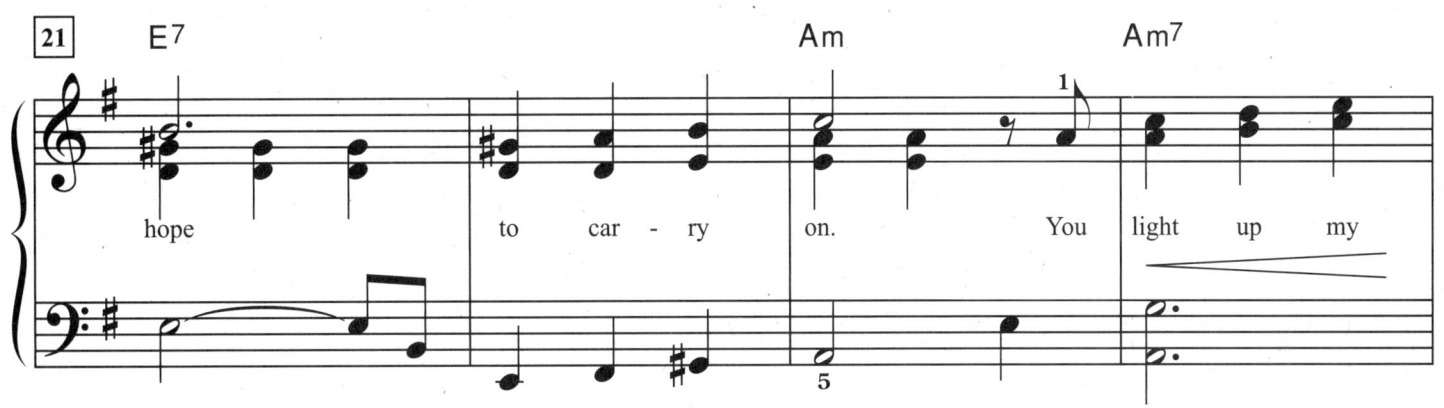
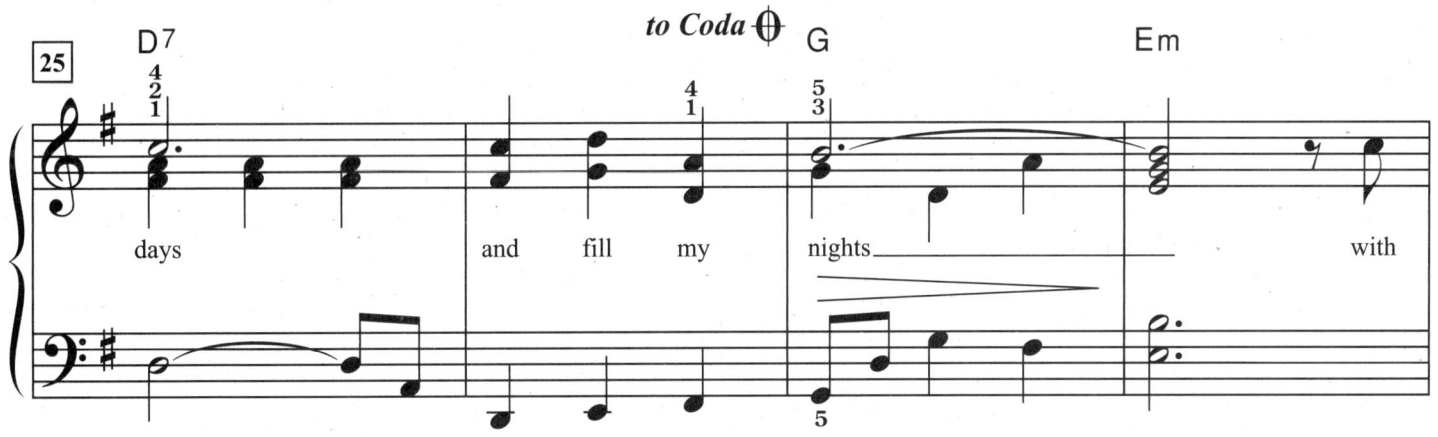
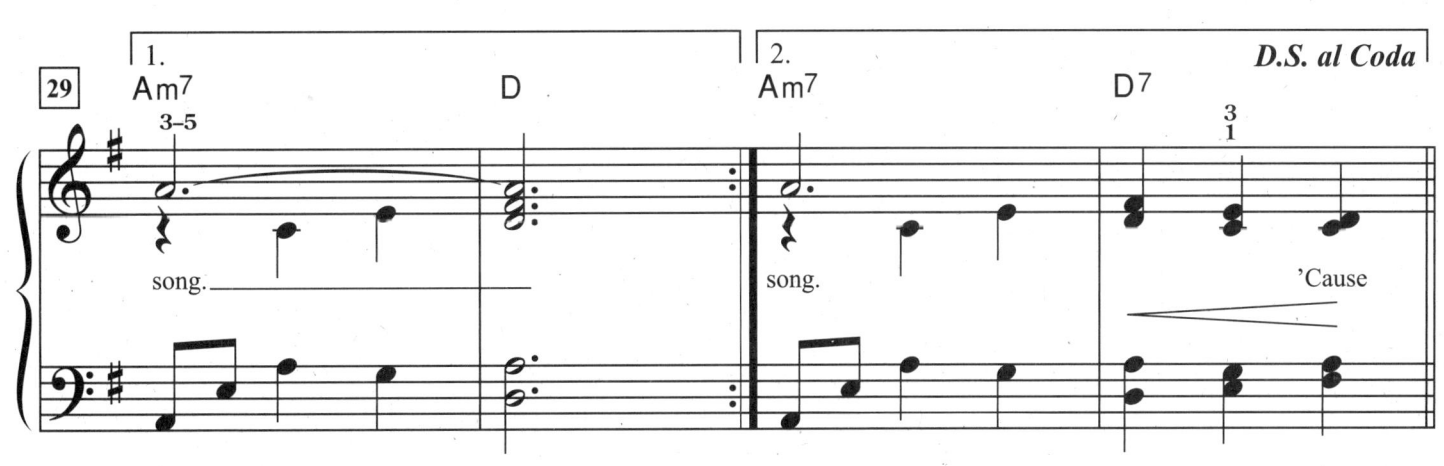

Coda
B B7 Em
nights with song.
f
36
A7 G/D B7 Em
It can't be wrong when it feels so right,
40
A7 G/D D7sus D7
mf
'cause you, you
mp
44
Slowly
C G D C G/B Am7 G
light up my life.
rit.
mf

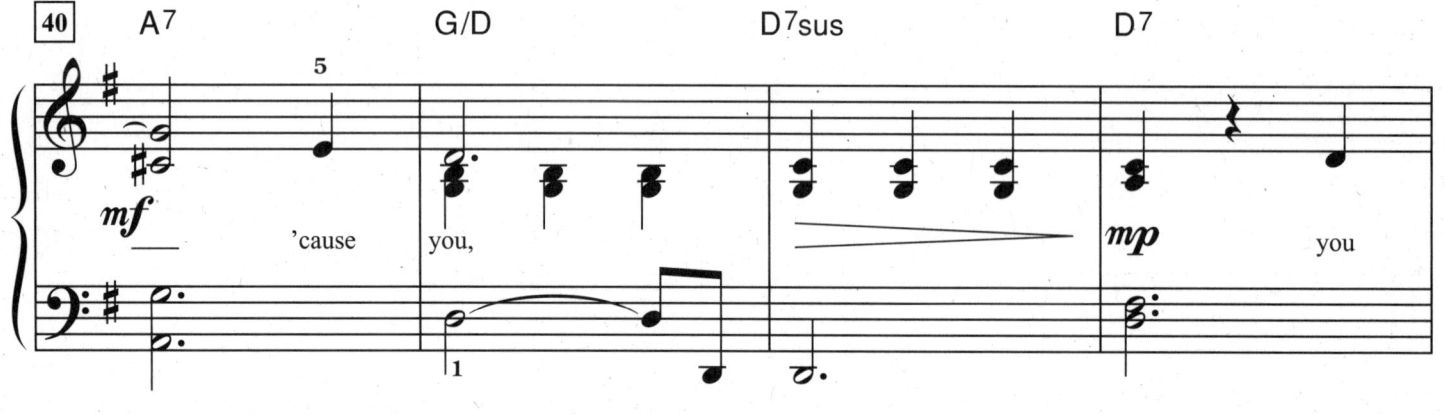

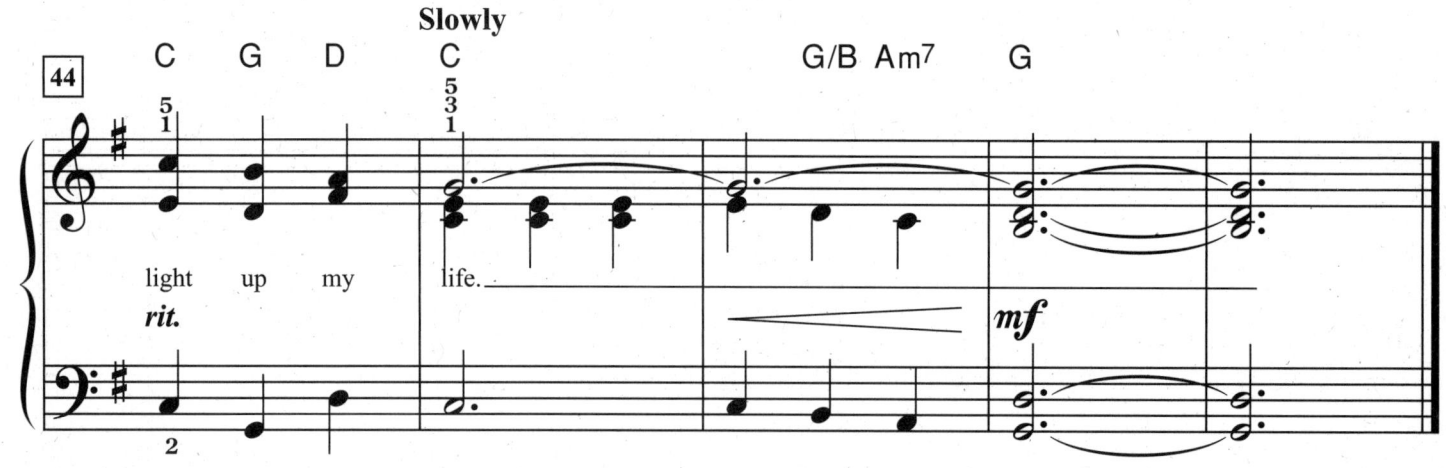

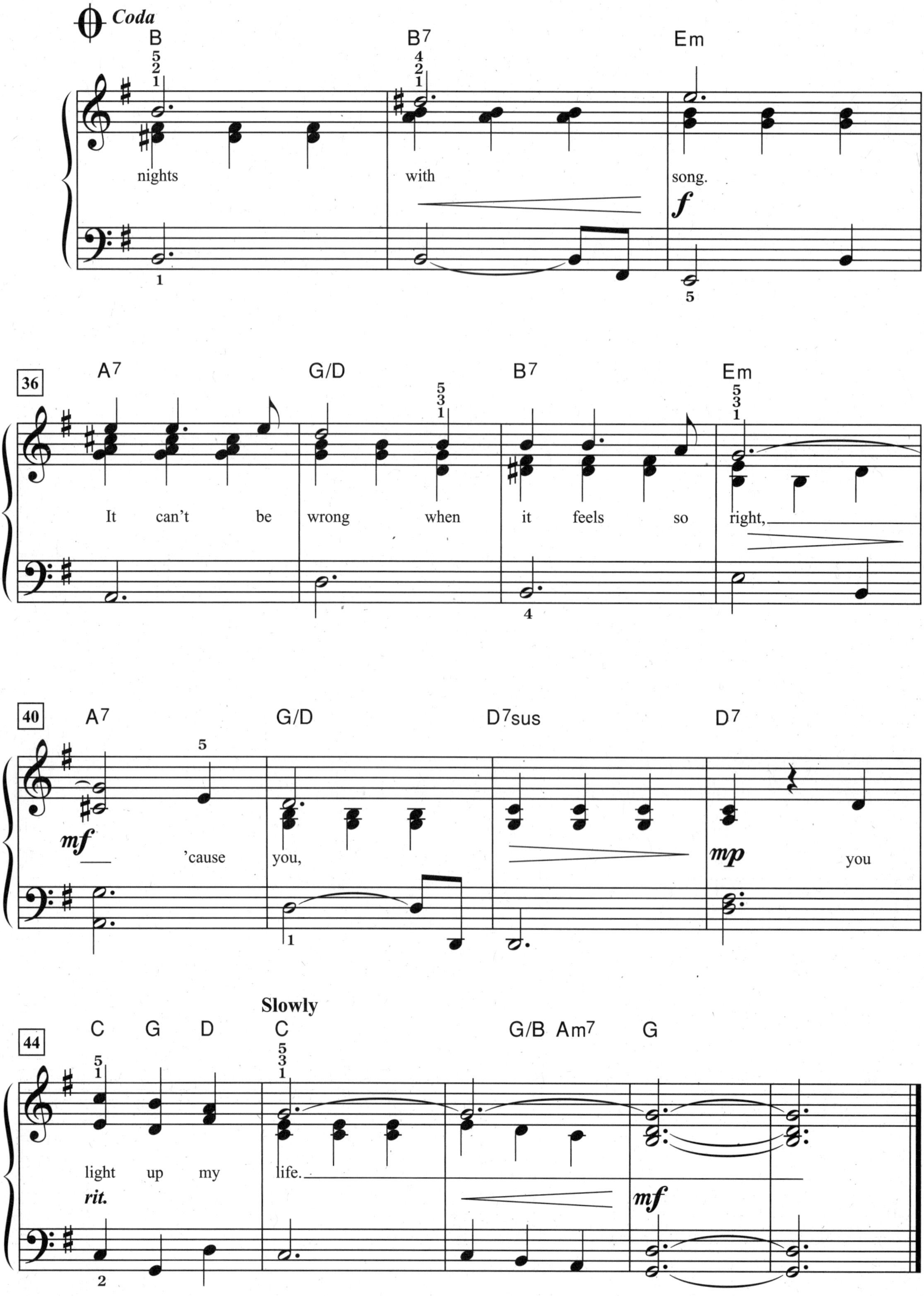

YOU RAISE ME UP

Words and Music by
Rolf Lovland and Brendan Graham
Arranged by Dan Coates

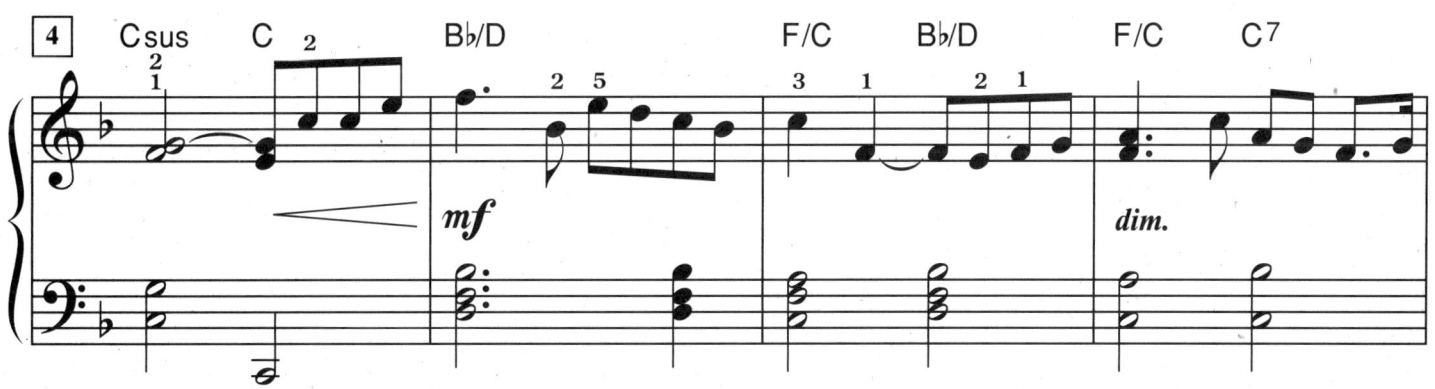

When I am down and oh, my soul, so

© 2002 UNIVERSAL MUSIC PUBLISHING, A Division of UNIVERSAL MUSIC AS and PEERMUSIC (Ireland) LTD.
All Rights for ROLF LOVLAND and UNIVERSAL MUSIC PUBLISHING administered in the U.S. and Canada by UNIVERSAL-POLYGRAM
INTERNATIONAL PUBLISHING, INC. (Publishing) and ALFRED MUSIC PUBLISHING CO., INC. (Print)
All Rights Reserved

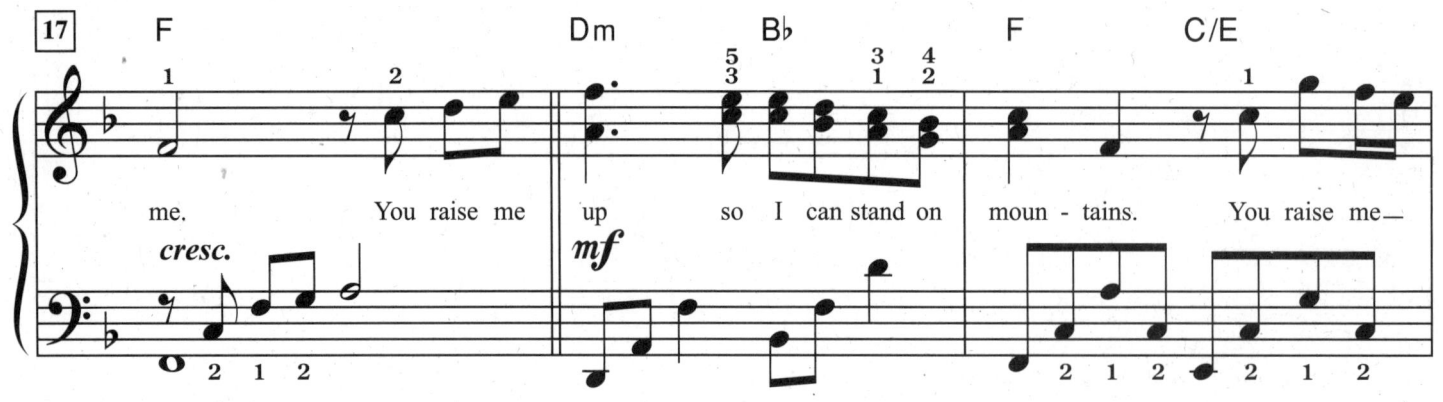
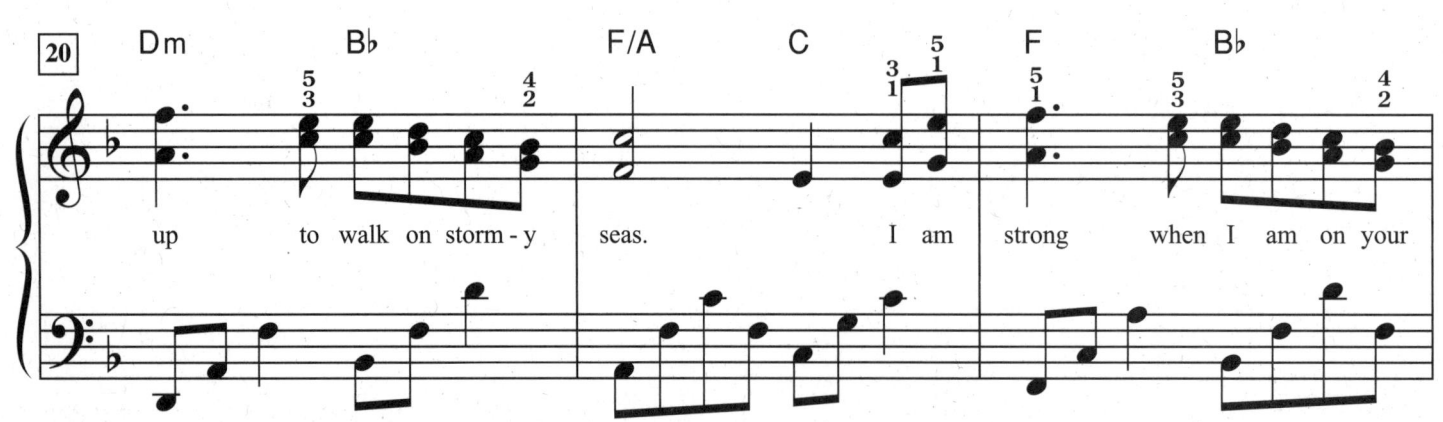

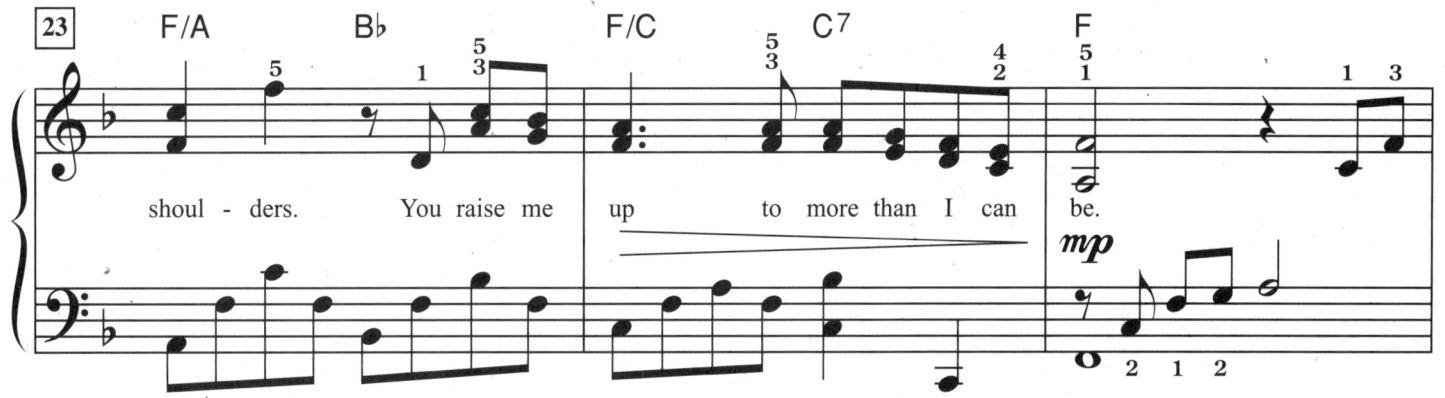
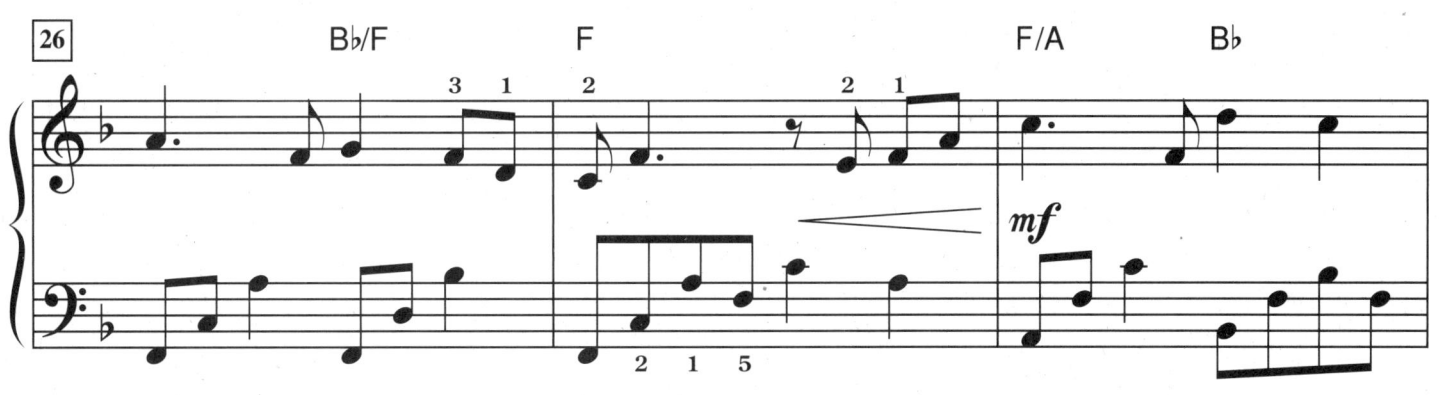
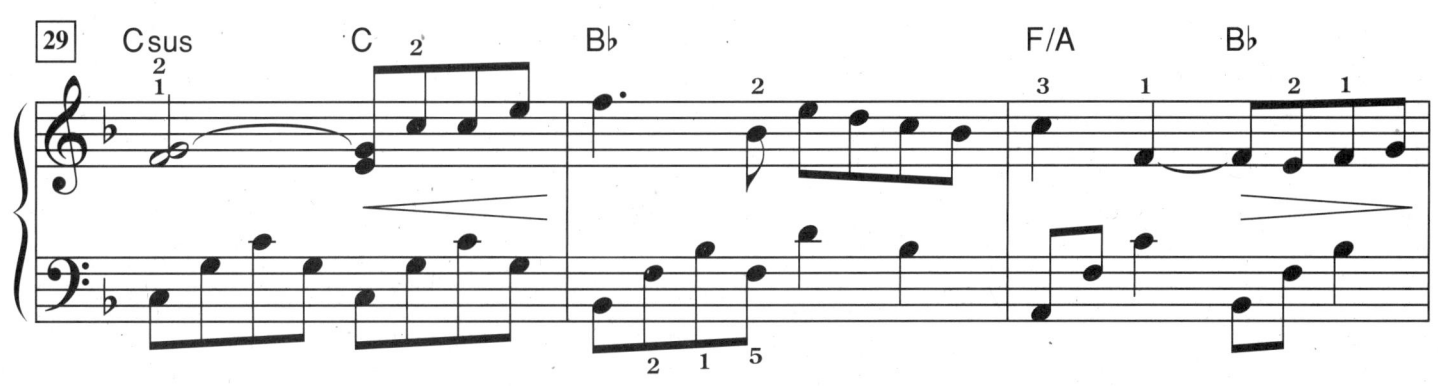
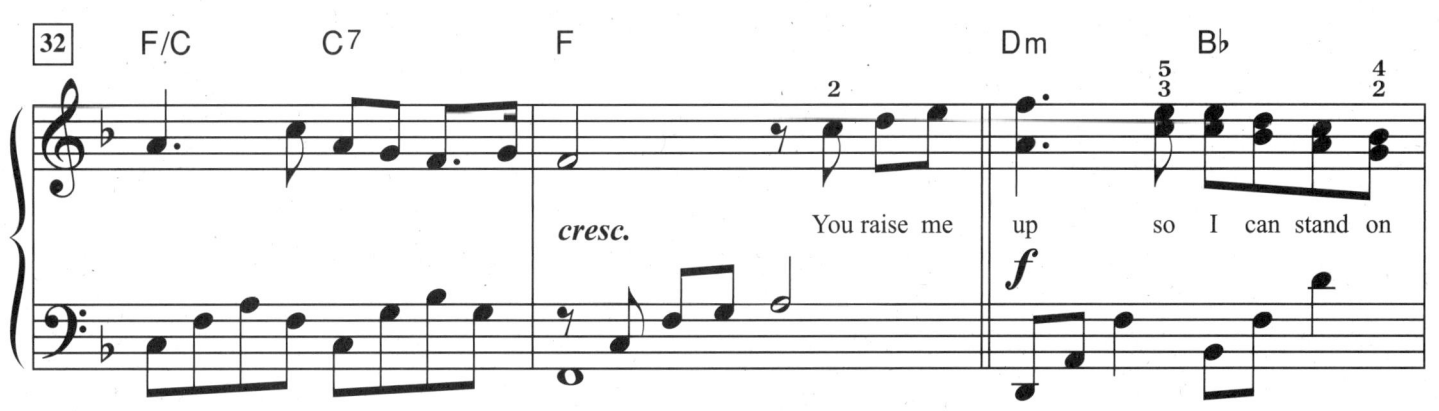

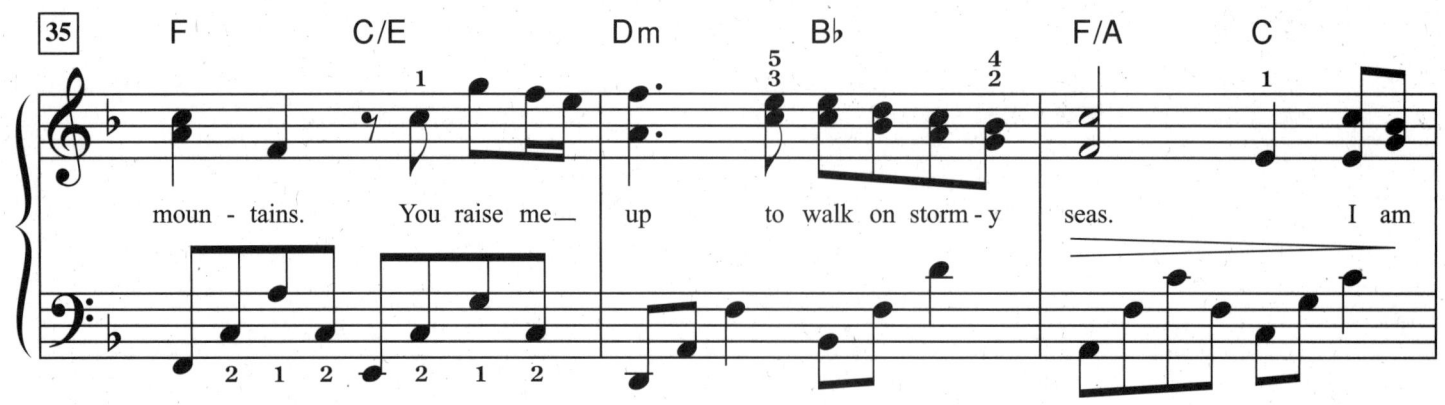
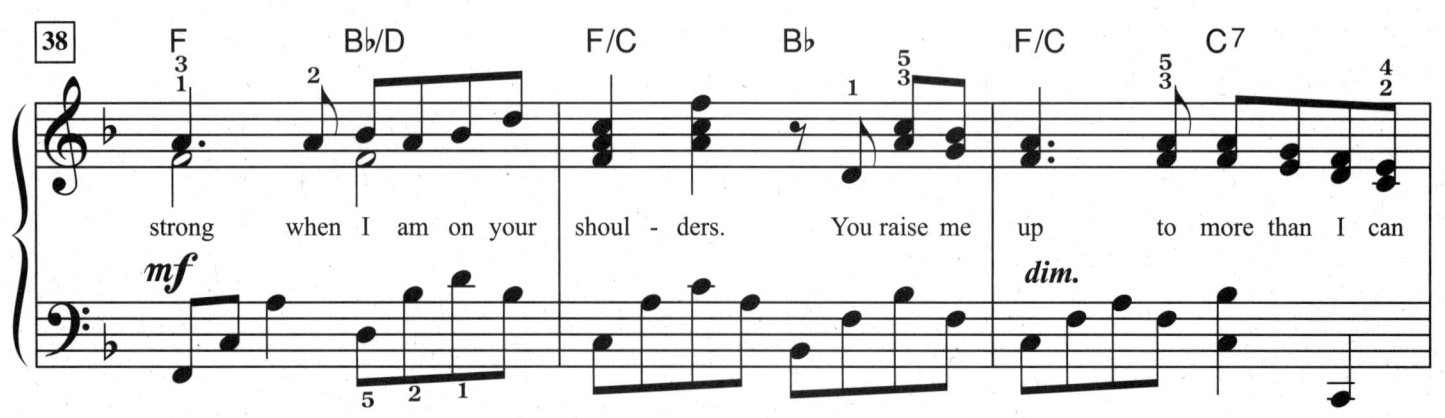

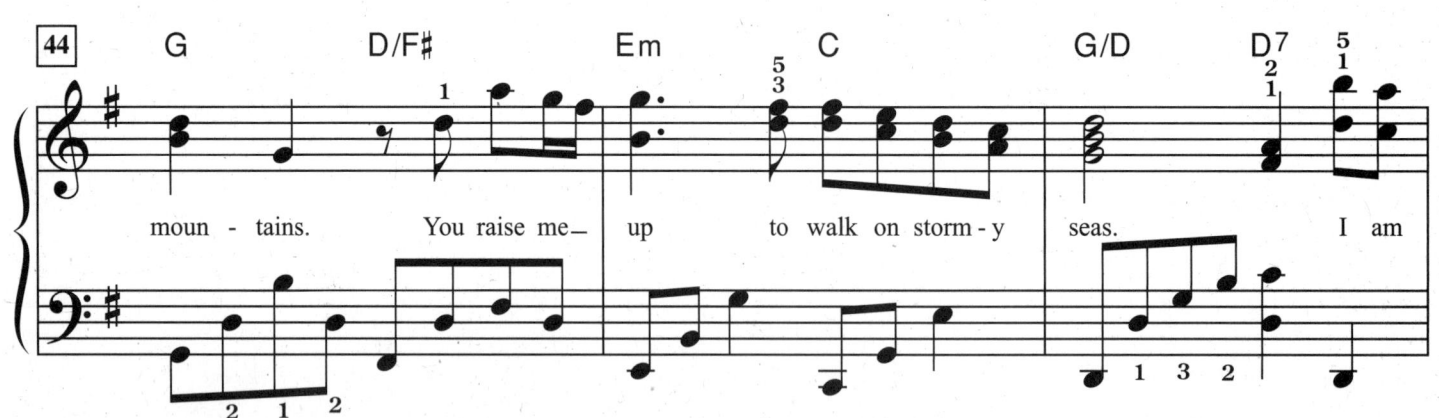

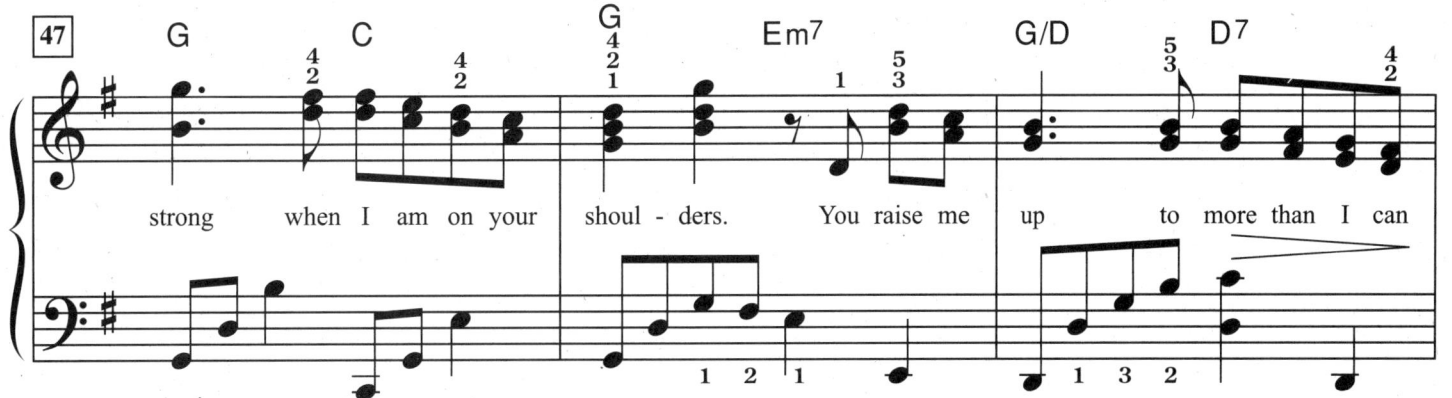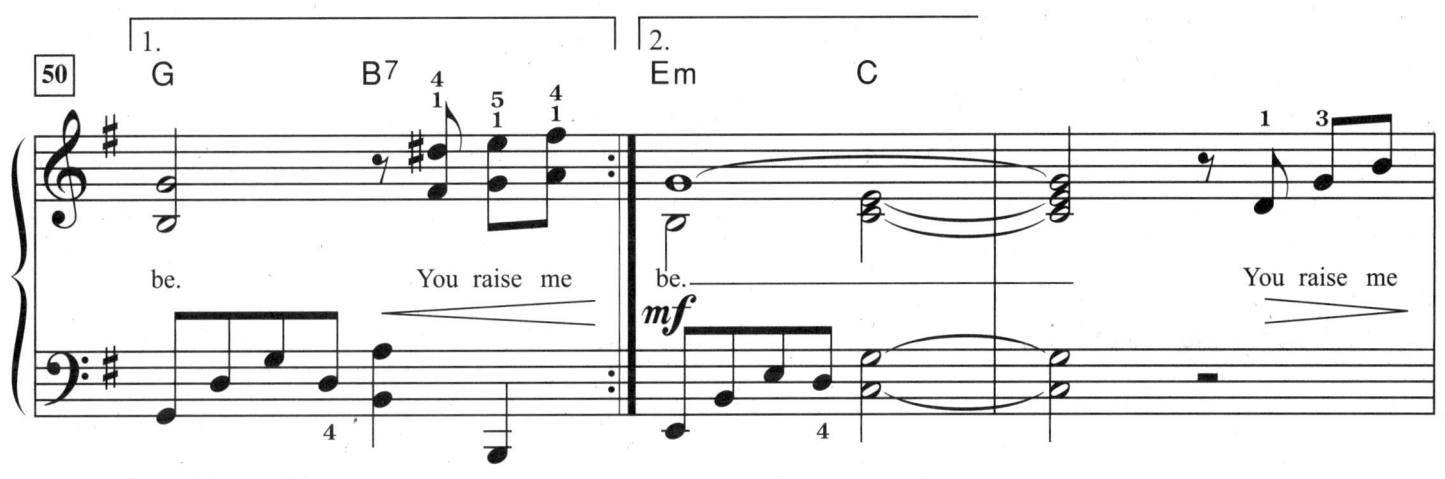

THE PRAYER

Words and Music by
Carole Bayer Sager and David Foster
Arranged by Dan Coates

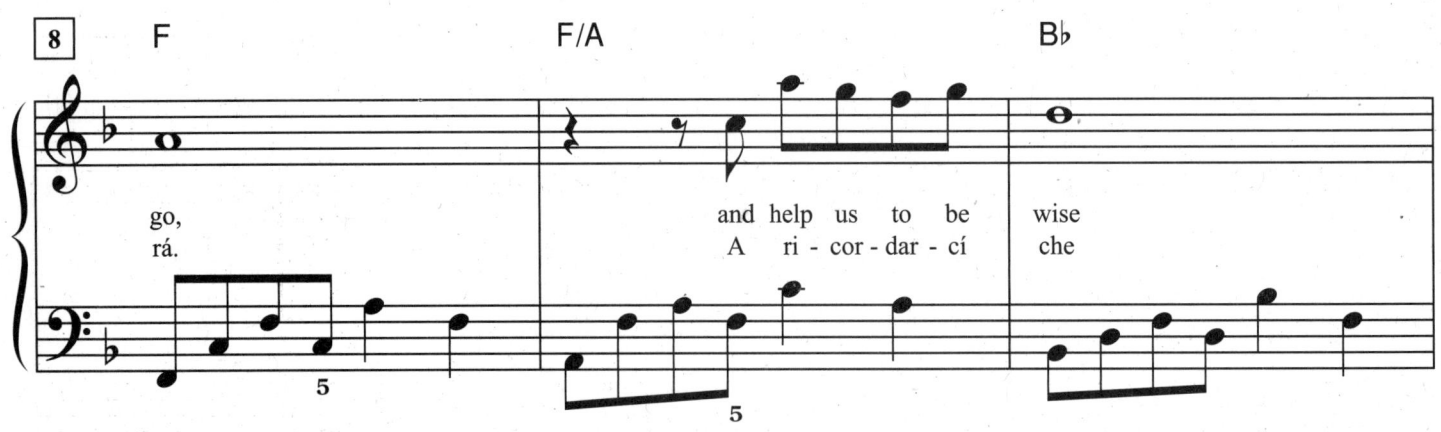

© 1998 WARNER-BARHAM MUSIC LLC (BMI)
All Rights Administered by SONGS OF UNIVERSAL, INC. (BMI)
Exclusive Worldwide Print Rights Administered by ALFRED MUSIC PUBLISHING CO., INC.
All Rights Reserved

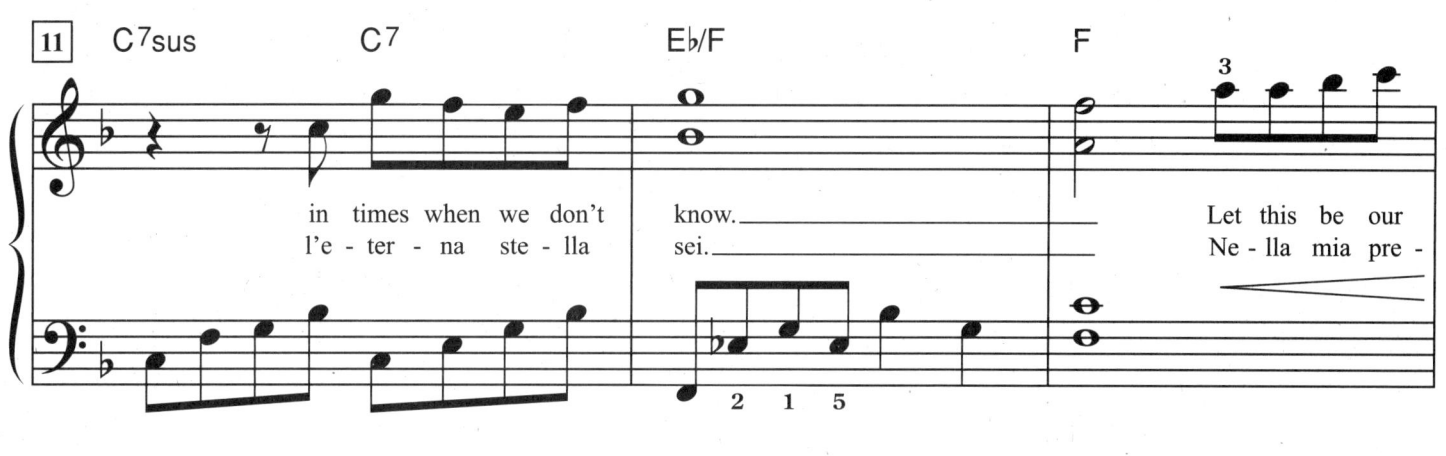
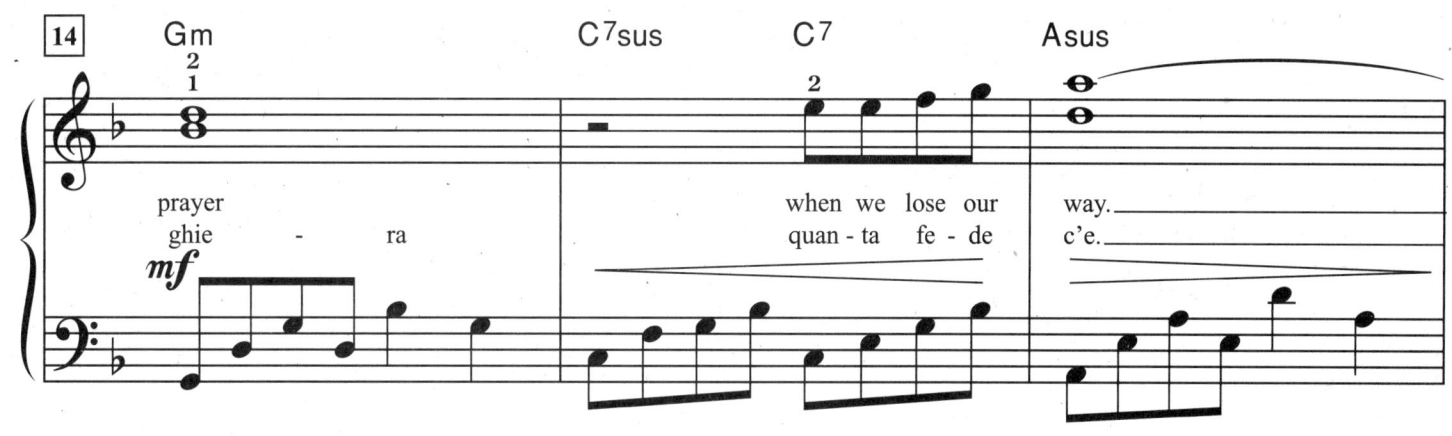

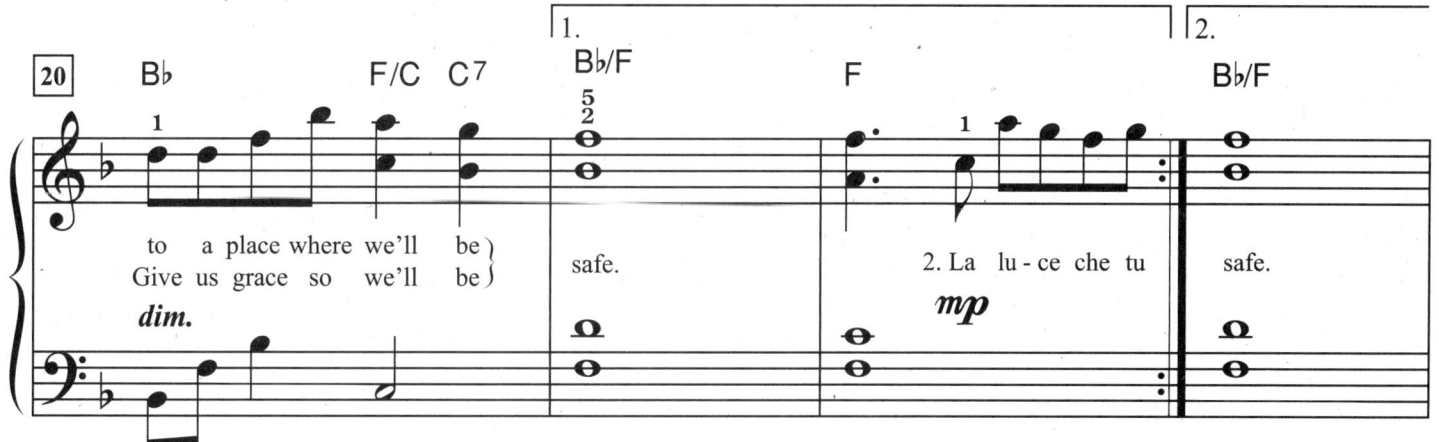

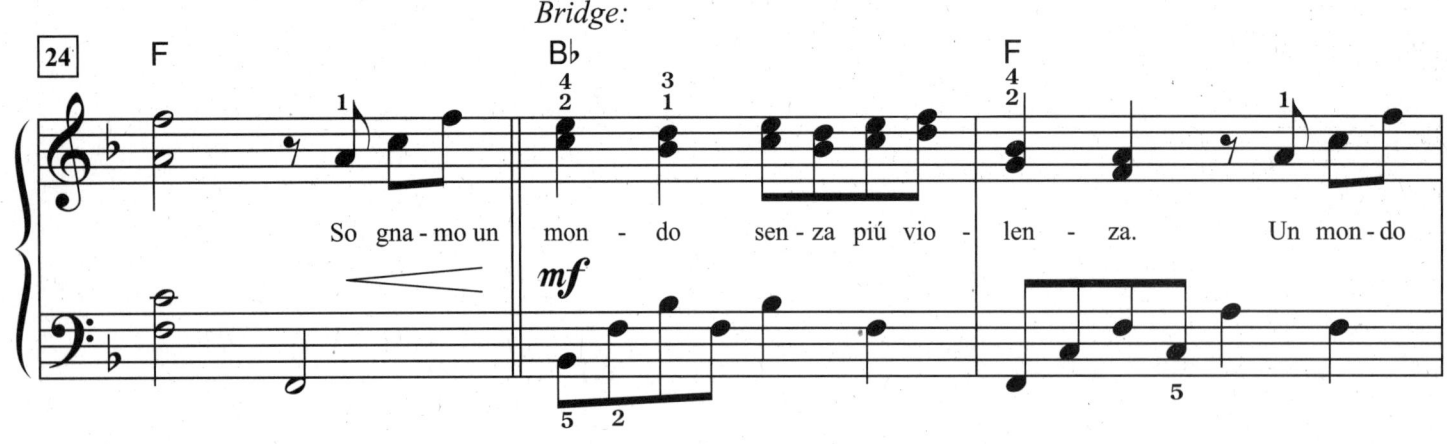
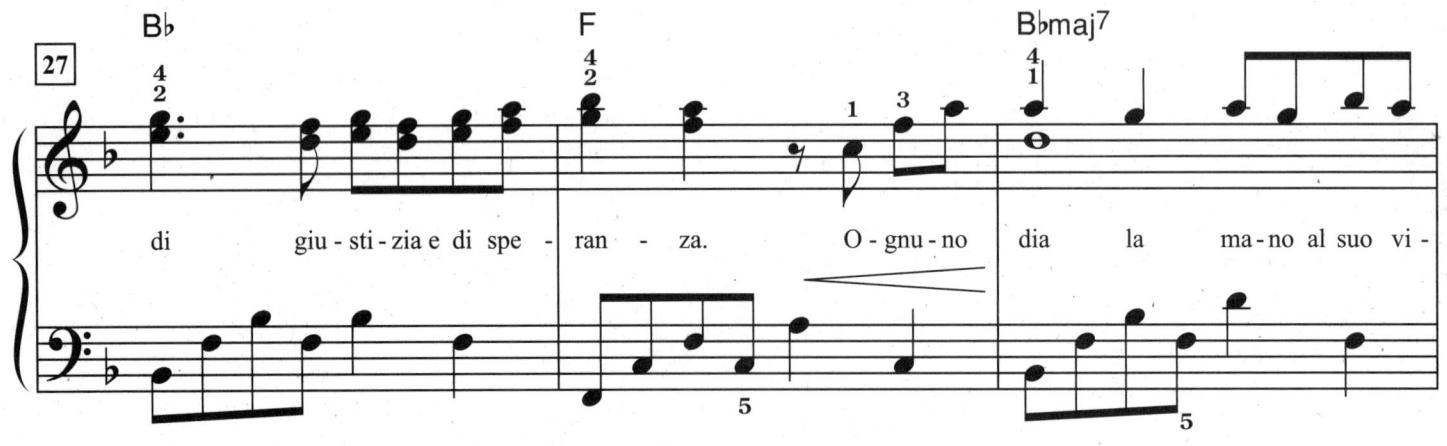
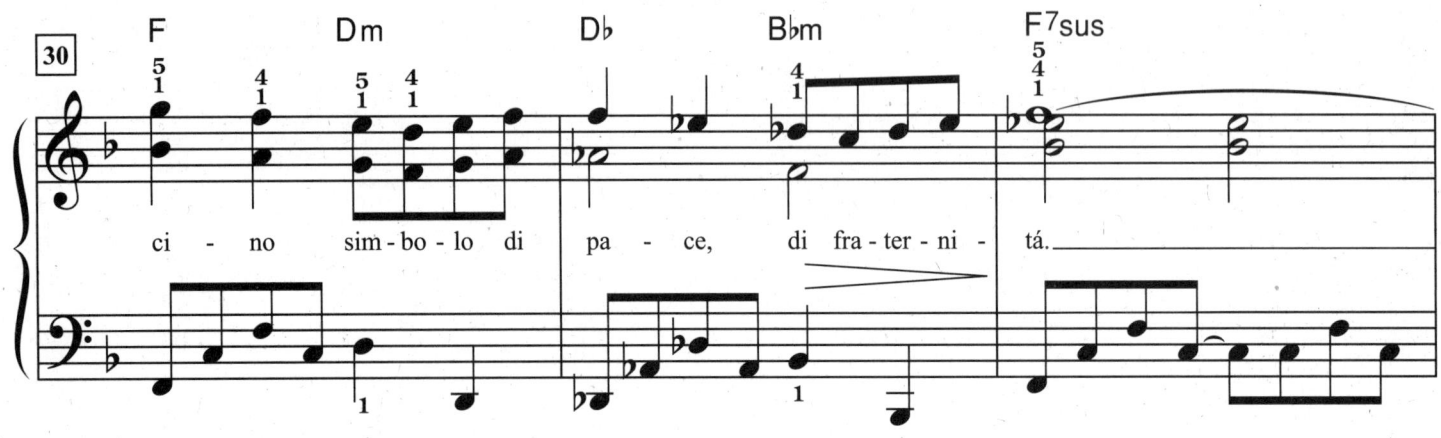

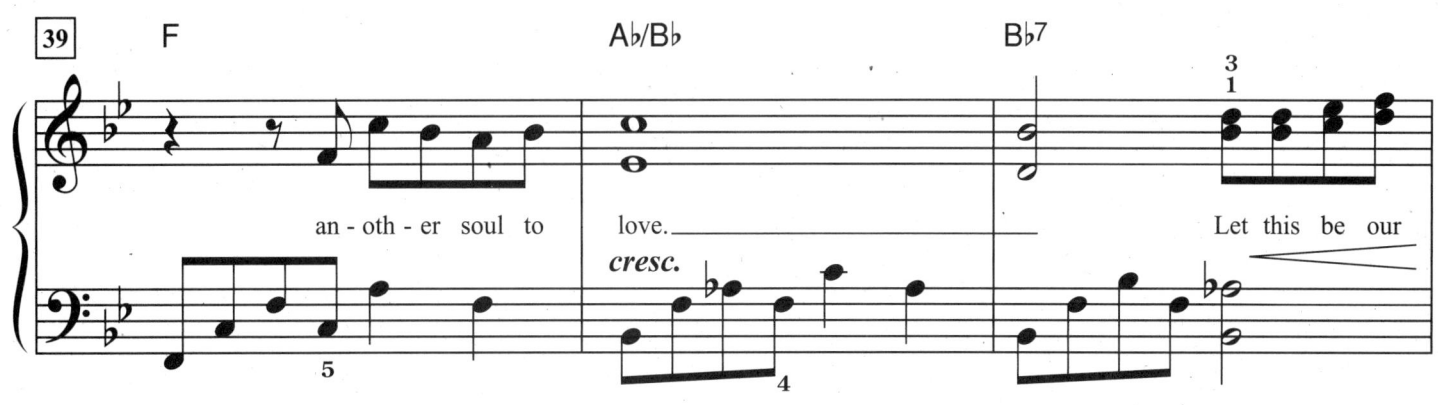
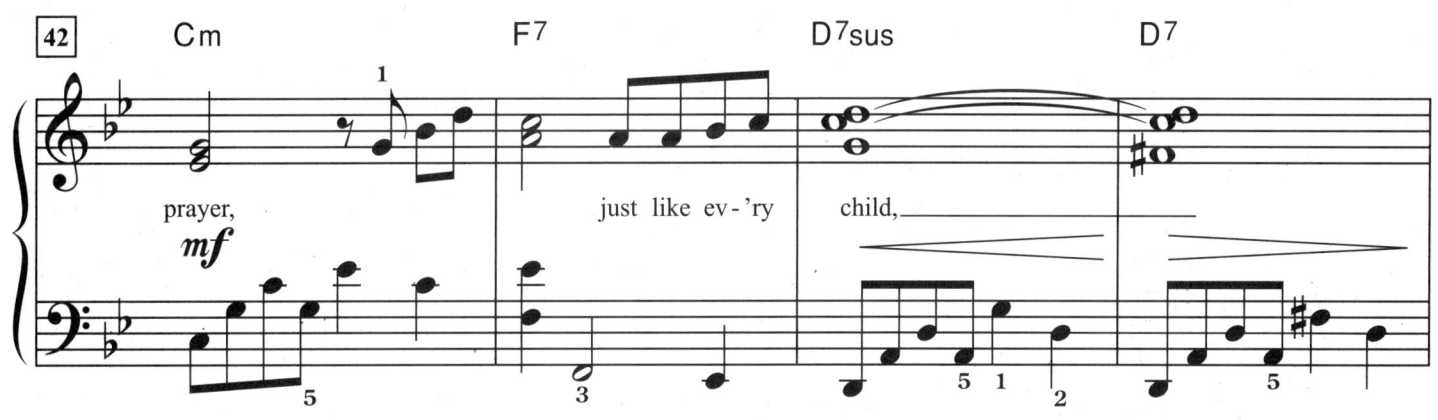

Verse 2 (English lyric):
I pray we'll find your light,
And hold it in our hearts
When stars go out each night.
Let this be our prayer,
When shadows fill our day.
Lead us to a place,
Guide us with your grace.
Give us faith so we'll be safe.

Verse 3 (Italian lyric):
La forza che ci dai
é il desiderio che.
Ognuno trovi amore
Intorno e dentro sé.